The Eagle and the Rising Sun

The Eagle
and the Rising Sun

AMERICANS
AND THE NEW RELIGIONS OF JAPAN

by

Robert S. Ellwood, Jr.

THE WESTMINSTER PRESS
Philadelphia

Book Design by Dorothy Alden Smith

Published by The Westminster Press®
Philadelphia, Pennsylvania

PRINTED IN THE UNITED STATES OF AMERICA

Library of Congress Cataloging in Publication Data

Ellwood, Robert S., 1933–
  The Eagle and the Rising Sun.

  Includes bibliographical references.
  1. Japan—Religion—1945–   2. United States
—Religion—1945–   1. Title.
BL2209.E44   299'.56   74–7317
ISBN 0–664–20707–3

FOR GRACIA FAY
With thoughts of the year in Japan

Contents

Foreword   9

1. The East Moves West   11

2. Tenrikyo,
   The Religion of Heavenly Wisdom   37

3. Nichiren Shoshu of America   69

4. The Church of World Messianity   111

5. Seicho-no-Ie,
   The House of Growth   147

6. Perfect Liberty   178

7. The Japanese New Religions
   and American Culture   206

   Addresses of Groups   215

   Notes   217

   Index   221

Foreword

Two major countries could scarcely be more diverse in cultural heritage than the United States of America and Japan. Both are nations that emerged rather late in the history of civilization. America is the heir of that stream of European philosophy, religion, and culture which stems from Athens and Jerusalem, and Japan of the quite different stream of East Asian civilization with its roots in India and China. One would not easily confuse the language, writing, art, rituals, or, in many cases, values of traditional Japan with those of Europe and America.

But one of the great facts of the twentieth century has been the discovery by Japan and the United States that, as remote from each other as they may have seemed in the past, they are now neighbors across the Pacific. From now on, the life and destiny of each is inseparably linked to the other. In tragic conflict, as major trading partners, as increasingly equal world powers, the two lands have been bound together like twins, each of whom—despite or even because of occasional bitterness—can never forget, nor even live without, the other. Where this kind of relationship exists, cultural influence is sure to follow geopolitical and economic interdependence.

This book is an attempt to explore one small but fascinating area of this cultural interpenetration—the impact in America of five groups numbered among the "New Religions" of Japan. This study has brought together two long-standing interests of mine: Japanese religion and new religious movements in America. The book reflects a series of experiences I have had with the members and activities of these groups. I hope it reflects something of the enjoyment and understanding which this encounter brought to me.

Invariably, I found the leaders and members of the groups I visited kind, patient, extremely helpful, and appreciative of my interest. I wish to express my deepest gratitude to all those who devoted hours of time to assisting me with this project. I wish to thank also the officials of each of the groups discussed for generous gifts of literature and for permission to quote therefrom. While the descriptions in this book represent the perceptions of an outsider striving to combine objectivity, sympathetic understanding, and personal interpretation, and may not in every case correspond exactly to the self-understanding of members of these groups, I sincerely hope the tone of my writing reflects the gratitude I feel for their many kindnesses to me.

R.S.E.

1

The East Moves West

I

It was a steamy summer night in 1962 on the island of Okinawa. I was talking in a Marine Corps officers quarters with a major who had been in Japan back in the early postwar years. Stationed near the ancient capital, Nara, he was one of those millions of postwar Americans who has had the unlikely experience of living for a short part of his life amid glittering pagodaed temples and dragon-roofed Oriental palaces set like carbuncles in fairyland gardens. The major told me that his residence was not far from the park-like headquarters of Tenrikyo, one of the Japanese New Religions. The "headquarters" is really an entire metropolis, Tenri City, devoted to the faith. It embraces schools, lodges, a world-famous museum, a great university, as well as a monumental temple with a vast courtyard.

The American officer confided how much he admired the faithful of this religion. Not only was he impressed with the magnitude of their architectural achievements, but he commented on the spotless cleanliness of the immense temple site, and the swarms of blue-coated volunteers who came every day to sweep and polish the grounds and buildings. Often, he said, he had gone out to help them, a strapping blond giant swinging a broom amid an army of short, dark, blue-coated devotees of an Asian faith.

But the major added that, though the spirit of Tenrikyo was so splendid that he would have liked to join it, when he looked at its sacred books he sadly realized he couldn't: the conceptual gap between East and West was too great.

In the years since, many Occidental Americans have had similar experiences. But in increasing numbers they have gone on to experience something more: that it is possible for East and West to meet in themselves. They have joined a religion that has come from Japan.

The first to come was Zen, a form of Buddhism that had roots in China and was brought to Japan in the Middle Ages. It emphasizes realization of the inner Buddha-nature, timeless and conceptless, empty and marvelous, through quiet meditation or through brain-cracking koans or puzzles. Sparked by the writings of D. T. Suzuki and his Western admirers such as Alan Watts and Christmas Humphreys, Zen became something of a vogue in the 1950's on campuses and in flats where pre–psychedelic "beatniks" drank cheap wine and listened to jazz and read such novels as Kerouac's *Dharma Bums*. Now in the 1970's, books on Zen still sell and there are ten or twelve excellent Zen centers in the United States.[1]

But in the 1960's, even as the American spiritual counter-culture exfoliated into a hundred exotic blossoms where before there had been little else than Zen, several other Japanese faiths entered America as options. The others, unlike Zen, were in the category known as the New Religions of Japan. These are faiths which have come into being, at least in their present "export" forms, within the last hundred years or so, and are products of Japan's encounter with modernity and with the West, even though they also revitalize certain very ancient motifs of Japanese religion.

Five of these Japanese New Religions have had some success in attracting converts among Americans of Occidental ancestry in the United States. They have thus played a part in the spiritual ferment of the 1960's and 1970's. At the same time, they have had an important role in the Japanese-American community. The one mentioned above, Tenrikyo, has been present in Japanese-American society since the 1920's; the other four did not appear on American shores in their present form until around 1960.

This book is about these five and their interaction with Americans of Occidental descent. Three other Japanese New Religions, at least, have been present in this country for some time: Konkokyo, Reiyukai, and Gedatsu. But since they do not seem to have made much impact outside the Japanese-American community, I have not included chapters on them, although I have heard that Gedatsu, a group related to esoteric Buddhism with its gorgeous rituals, has drawn some attenders among Latin Americans. The colorful "Dancing Religion" (Odori Shukyo, officially Tensho Kotai Jingu Kyo) has made several vigorous efforts to penetrate the American counter-culture, most recently in the San Francisco Bay area, but does not seem yet to have put down deep roots in the New World.

II

The genesis and growth of the New Religions of Japan is one of the most remarkable phenomena of recent religious history. Although most of the major examples have roots in the nineteenth and early twentieth centuries, they burst into prominence after the Second World War. The collapse of the old order with its traditional Shinto and Buddhist structures, and of the more recently imposed nationalistic Shinto uniting throne and altar, left a spiritual vacuum. The new genuine religious freedom made it possible for people to shift allegiances as they wished. In this situation, a set of groups that had long seemed small, disreputable, and harassed grew with explosive force.

By 1960 approximately one in five Japanese was connected with one of them; by 1970 about one in three, if the full reported membership of three Nichiren Buddhist groups closely related to the New Religions is counted.

But the overall shape of the world of the New Religions was demarcated by the late 1950's. In his 1963 book, *The New Religions of Japan*,[2] Harry Thomsen stated that there were 171 groups of the New Religions type, but selected only fifteen as being important enough to warrant detailed treatment. Today the same fifteen, which include the five treated here, remain the most prominent. Most of them are by now at least in the second generation of leadership, have arrived at a stabilized doctrinal, worship, and organizational profile, and are growing at only a sedate rate. Thus, it is as fairly mature, rationalized institutions that they have entered America. (See H. Byron Earhart's *The New Religions of Japan: A Bibliography of Western-Language Materials*, Sophia University, Tokyo, 1970, for guides to further reading on the New Religions.)

Each of them has much in common with the others, which sets apart the New Religions as a group. To understand what their common qualities are, let us construct the history of an imaginary faith of the New Religion type.

First imagine an intense and unusual individual, probably of peasant background. He or she has undergone a life of privation and suffering, wracked by want, sickness, and the death of children. Then the individual has a breakthrough experience—perhaps on a mountaintop, perhaps on a streetcar or in a farmhouse—in which a deity, probably out of timeless Japanese folk religion, or Buddhism, or Occidental spiritualism, seizes and speaks to the oppressed one, assuring him or her that there is really but this one God, and he or she is selected as the deity's one envoy.

The visionary tells his neighbors of his experiences. Many scoff, but some are convinced, perhaps because of the radiant intensity and conviction of the preacher, perhaps because something in the message makes sense of a world shattered by hardship, economic troubles, and disturbing changes in the social order. The new message puts the pieces of the puzzle together in a way that makes some people say, "This was really true all the time, but we didn't realize it until he told us."

The message will be basically that there is one God, and that he is working in the world. The world is now much disturbed, but that is because ours is a time of transition from one age to another. A day is coming when the world will be renewed and paradisal. Until then, God has set apart a select group of people to prepare the way for the New Age.

You can enter this group, the prophet says, and your life will be joyful and full of meaning, where once it was drab and oppressed. Spirits and God himself will speak to you through me. Moreover, I bring to you a practice—a chant, ritual, or method of meditation—by which the powers of the New Age can be applied now to heal your ills and renew your spirits. For all is really Mind, and the power of unshackled Mind can totally change for good yourself and your environment. Ours is a period of great change; through this faith you can be in on the changes, and even ahead of them.

Through the power of teachings like these the leader gathers around him a circle, and finally a denomination. In time the movement builds a splendid headquarters; the beauty of this site anticipates the delights of the coming New Age. When the leader finally ages and dies, the spiritual authority is passed on to a younger member of his family, although by then the day-to-day administrative leadership is in the hands of less-colorful bureaucrats who have established a well-honed doctrine, form of worship, organizational table, and financial system for the denomination. The latter is now able to support works overseas—in Brazil, Europe, and the United States.

This history has been followed almost exactly by all the groups discussed in this book except Nichiren Shoshu. That is in a slightly different case since in one sense its charismatic founder was Nichiren, back in the thirteenth century.

III

Thomsen divides the New Religions into three major groups: the "Old" New Religions, the Nichiren group, and the Omoto group. Of the five Japanese religions discussed in this book, one is in the first category, Tenrikyo; one, Nichiren Shoshu, is in the second; and three, Seicho-no-Ie, World Messianity, and Perfect Liberty, are in the third.

The "Old" New Religions have their origins in the nineteenth century. The two major groups of this set, Tenrikyo and Konkokyo, were registered by the Japanese government as Shinto sects until 1945. They have not only carried over much of the worship patterns of Shinto but have also served as prototypes of many other New Religions.

Both Tenrikyo and Konkokyo were founded by individuals of peasant stock who felt themselves called out by a deity who became for them and their faith a monotheistic High God. In the case of Tenrikyo, a woman named Miki Nakayama[3] had been serving as a medium for a shamanistic healer trying to restore her son to health. When she was in trance, a divine being entered her, saying, "I am the True and Original God . . ."

Konkokyo was started by a farmer, Bunjiro Kawate, now known as Konko Daijin. In 1859 he had a revelation in which a folk religion deity of Taoistic background, Konjin, was renamed Tenchi-kane-no-kami ("God of gold in heaven and earth").

These two religions moved away from the traditional relativism of Shinto to an attitude of personal faith and devotion toward one God, mediated through one founder. In their powerful personalities, teachings, and production of new scriptures, Miki Nakayama and Konko Daijin provided their followers with unique and direct experiences of the one God. There were also in each case specific ways the experience was mediated: through a kind of personal confession in Konkokyo, through dancing rituals in Tenrikyo.

This personalization of religious experience gives a clue to understanding the New Religions phenomenon. The emphasis is placed far more directly than in conventional Shinto or Buddhism on subjectivity.

The period from the early nineteenth century to the middle, when Tenrikyo and Konkokyo originated, was a time of great crisis for Japan. First came economic failures,

with attendant hardship and even starvation in the countryside, as the old Tokugawa regime declined. Millions
lost savings large and small, hunger and disease were rampant, and everywhere the poor rose to demonstrate or riot.

Next, the black ships of the foreigners appeared in the
ports of the long-isolated island nation, demanding trade
and, some feared, colonial rule. The Tokugawa shoguns
were unable to handle the situation, and in 1868 an alliance of nobles arose to overthrow the shoguns and nomi-
nally restore direct rule by the Emperor, actually rule
through him by a coterie determined to modernize Japan
at all costs.

If these changes were not enough to convince countless
Japanese that one age was passing and that another, full
of combined hope and fearsome uncertainty, was dawning,
the rapid extension of telegraph wires, railway tracks, and
recruiting offices for the new European-style Imperial
Army was.

The modernization experience shatters personality and
life-style patterns shaped by immemorial custom, the sea-
sonal cycle, family and community, shrine and temple. It
seems to invalidate or make inaccessible the former supports that an individual had in his joys and sorrows, and
leaves him far more vulnerable to his subjectivity, to his
moods and feelings, hopes and dreams, as a separate person. The New Religions, which arose in the context of that
nineteenth-century Japanese experience and burgeoned in
the aftermath of the new trauma of 1945, offer new groups
and new ways through which people can handle the shocks
of rapid change. They echo a major theme of modernity
everywhere by isolating the feelings, decisions, guilt and
repentance, doubt and belief, of the individual. They make
these personal subjective states important, rather than

the traditional communal practices in which individuality is submerged such as lighting a new fire at New Year's or doing a village circle dance at the August Obon festival to welcome back the spirits of the dead.

But in times like those in which the New Religions arose, it is necessary for many people to find an identity within themselves, an identity validated by their own feelings rather than by family or status in a traditional social structure. If one's relationship to God is the ultimate definer of who one is, they want to be able to say, "I know by feelings within me how God can be reached, regardless of what happens in the outside world or what anyone else says," rather than, "I want to do it this way because this is the way my people have always done it." The New Religions offer techniques through which one can make the first statement. Indeed, they almost come to say that subjectivity is all—through his thoughts one makes his world.

IV

The Nichiren group of New Religions, however, shows that this crisis and discovery is no new thing in Japan. From the eighth to the eleventh century, Japan had been ruled from a court at Heian (modern Kyoto), which enjoyed a delightful life of love and poetry and had close ties with ancient esoteric Buddhist monasteries on mountaintops but grew increasingly distant toward the toiling common people. Finally warlords from the provinces overthrew the old regime and established their own government in the city of Kamakura. It was a time of calamity upon calamity, and of the shattering of traditional form in society and religion alike.

The new men of Kamakura wanted new forms of Buddhism, simplified forms for the man facing death on the field of battle or for the bookless peasant or the merchant busy in his shop, not a Buddhism available only to the leisured elegant courtier or the cloistered monk. Several new streamlined Buddhisms arose proposing a simple key to the rewards of faith anyone could apply: Pure Land Buddhism, with its promise of salvation to any who just called on the name of Amida Buddha; Zen, with its simple meditation; and the Buddhism of Nichiren, who encapsulated all of Buddhism in the Lotus Sutra and the chant "*Nam Myoho Renge Kyo.*" Of all the teachers of Kamakura Buddhism, none was more fiery, enigmatic, or influential than Nichiren.

Yet from the thirteenth through the early twentieth century the Nichiren sects enjoyed a fairly quiet life, offering little promise of the fantastic power that Nichiren's Buddhism was to display after 1945. But in postwar Japan, Nichiren-related sects, especially Nichiren Shoshu, grew with phenomenal speed, thanks to the work of a militant layman's organization, Sokagakkai. While technically not an independent religious group, it has functioned much like the other New Religions, and even more successfully.

Through its work the old Nichiren Shoshu denomination has been thoroughly revitalized, and its contemporary message—in Japan and even more in America—has been consistent with the basic themes of the New Religions. Central to its teaching, for example, is the motif that through chanting one releases his potential for joyous, creative thought which can change both himself and his environment.

Two other Nichiren-related New Religions, Reiyukai and Rissho Kosei Kai, number their adherents in Japan in the millions, but have less importance in America.

V

Finally, there is the Omoto group. Omoto, meaning "great source," is the name of a New Religion founded at the beginning of the century by a farm woman called Nao Deguchi (1836–1918) and her son-in-law and adoptive son, Onisaburo Deguchi (1871–1948). In her earlier years, Nao suffered a life of extreme hardship from poverty. Moreover, her husband died young, and of her eight children seven died, ran away, or became insane. She became a worker for Konkokyo. Finally, in 1892, when she seemed at the end of all hope, she experienced a vision in which the Konkokyo deity told her that the dissolution of the world was at hand, that God would send a savior, and that the kingdom of heaven would soon be built upon this earth.

When in 1898 Nao met Onisaburo, a scholar, mystic, and spiritualist of humble birth, she was convinced he was the Promised One. Together they started the sect later called Omoto. It produced lengthy scriptures. The *Ofudesaki* (not to be confused with the Tenrikyo book of the same name) was written by Nao during the last twenty-seven years of her life, and claimed to be direct dictations of the Spirit of God. Its central theme is the advent of the New World expected by Omoto.

The *Reikai Monogatari* ("Tales of the Spirit World") was dictated from out of trance by Onisaburo. It expounds God as the one reality, the existence of both a spiritual and a material world, the creation of man in the spirit world and his temporary descent into matter. While compatible with much Oriental tradition, the doctrine also has close parallels to the teachings of Swedenborg and many

Spiritualists in the West, and reflects this Occidental influence.

Omoto reached a high point in the 1920's. It claimed several million members, and the colorful Onisaburo Deguchi, who did not shrink from virtually identifying himself with God and the Emperor and who voiced outspoken social criticism, was at the height of his power. But later, owing both to government harassment and the death of the two founders, Omoto diminished, reporting 144,000 members in 1970.

But the founders of two New Religions that are now prominent—Taniguchi of Seicho-no-Ie and Okada of World Messianity—were at one time workers for Omoto. Taniguchi, in fact, was one of the scribes who recorded the *Reikai Monogatari*. There is no direct connection between Omoto and Perfect Liberty, but some ideas seem close to Omoto patterns of thought.

Indeed, the oceanic Omoto texts have been an unfailing fountain of inspiration for many religious leaders. Among them, World Messianity's Okada emphasized the Omoto theme of the coming in of a luminous New Age heralded by a messiah, the interaction of this world with the spirit world, and the concept of the religion's headquarters as a paradisal foretaste of the New Age. Taniguchi picked up especially Omoto's mentalism, the idea that Mind is all and can create healing and joy, as well as some traces of spiritualistic inspiration. Perfect Liberty emphasizes the aestheticism which is also an Omoto theme—Onisaburo Deguchi said that God is the supreme artist and that everyone should have a form of artistic expression through which he manifests his potentialities and draws closer to the divine mind.

In addition, Onisaburo Deguchi's creative genius in religion brought forth a number of mystic rites, for healing, divination, and spirit communication, which have been taken up and modified by the other religions. As always in spiritualism, the fundamental motif is the power of the unfettered mind to soar beyond the confines of space and time to visit other realms and create its own universe by the power of thought.

VI

Some common characteristics shared by the New Religions are:

1. The New Religions are founded by strong, charismatic, shamanistic figures. In this respect, as Ichiro Hori has shown, they represent a renewal of a very ancient Japanese pattern.[4]

From the dawn of recorded time in Japan, and doubtless before that in the days of prehistoric hunters and farmers, select individuals have heard the summons of the gods and left field and village to ascend the weird heights of Japan's countless mountains. There they have done spiritual battle, fasting, chanting, going into trance, shaking with ecstasy, until heaven released to them power to heal and prophesy.

Shinto and Buddhism alike have had relationships with the tradition of mountain ascetics. Buddhist sages like Kobo Daishi, founder of the Shingon sect, and the Zen poet Basho drew strength from the mountains. But for the most part the tradition has been maintained by marginal but popular sects of both great faiths, and above all by the *yamabushi* ("mountain priests"). These colorful religionists were mainstays of popular faith down to the late nineteenth century, when they were largely suppressed.

In their heyday the *yamabushi* were organized into orders vaguely connected with Buddhist sects, but in practice were generally their own men. In the mountains, they initiated novices and disciplined themselves by walking on hot coals, standing under waterfalls, and holding one another by the heels over towering cliffs for a "peek into eternity." Then they would return to villages to make a living as faith healers and magicians, often marrying a medium who would serve as associate. Konko Daijin and Onisaburo Deguchi both seem to have had a shamanistic experience directly; Onisaburo even tells of spending about a week on Mt. Takakura and being granted there mystical revelations.

In Japan, the line between the divine and the recipient of divine authority is always thin; most of the founders of New Religions have been virtually deified after death. Partly because of belief in the special charisma of the founder, and partly after the model of similar practice in Japanese business, government, and even academic life, the leadership of the New Religions is usually kept in the founder's family. Of the five groups under consideration, all except Nichiren Shoshu have established a line of succession in the founder's family. Typically, administrative authority goes to other hands, but a son or a daughter or other relative of the founder is highly exalted as spiritual center, and blesses, teaches, and perhaps imparts new revelations. Sometimes, in typical Japanese manner, the succession is assured by marriage and adoption rather than blood lineage, but the principle is maintained. Thus there is a monarchical quality about the New Religions somewhat alien to American expectations.

2. All the New Religions emphasize belief in one God, or in the unity of the divine nature. This is probably of a piece with the concept of one authoritative divine spokes-

man and one revelation. Probably it is partly influenced by Western religion. The idea of one God is in contrast to Shinto polytheism, although the way was prepared by the idea of one Buddha-nature which lay behind popular Buddhism's plethora of mediatory Buddhas and bodhi-sattvas, and by Confucianism and Taoism with their vaguely unitarian Heaven or Great Principle or Great Way.

3. The New Religions all show evidence of syncretism; ideas and philosophies from East and West have been taken, in a time of radical cultural confrontation, and combined into new mixes. Jesus is quoted as often as Buddha; the Western ideal of building Jerusalem here and now and making earth fair is joined with Eastern ideas such as reincarnation.

4. The New Religions anticipate a New Age of earthly joy coming through imminent divine action and foreshadowed in the experience of the founder and the communal life. This very important attitude engenders an intense optimism about the human future. While others today may pose as pessimists, they are hopeful and confident. Members feel they are ahead of the rest of the world, and share a marvelous secret not yet known to most of mankind.

5. Closely tied to this hope is the role of the sacred center. All the New Religions discussed in this book have lavish headquarters or training centers that are more than buildings and temples. Like Tenri City, most of them are whole model communities, replete with gorgeous architecture, splendid parks, lovely vistas, and exquisite landscaping. Members and others visiting them catch a vision of the coming New Age when the whole earth will be as beautiful and humane as this foretaste of the earthly paradise.

6. Pilgrimage to the sacred centers is always an impor-

tant feature of the New Religions. Members near and far, on their periodical, well-organized visits, learn something of the teaching, and more important, feel part of a magnificent, forward-looking, and vast spiritual army.

7. The New Religions have tight and thorough organization, generally. The individual has to take certain simple but definite steps to enter, and thus he appreciates that he has made a deliberate decision and commitment. He becomes a part of a local chapter which gives him responsibilities, support, and identity as a member of the movement. He has meetings to attend, things to do, and is inundated with a stream of publications. He is caught up in a participation mystique—the group not only may provide him his faith but also organizes much of his time and gives him his social life as well. In Japan, this is much in contrast to the traditional religions, which, except on the level of village life, tend to be rather remote spectacles for the masses of people who are not provided hereditary roles in temple or shrine. With the dislocation of traditional society by urbanization and industrialization in modern Japan, millions have been thrown as isolated individuals or nuclear families into the anonymity of modern cities. Young men, bachelors or newly married, leave the countryside to make Hondas or transistors in the cities, far from ancestral shrine or anyone who cares about them personally. Small shopkeepers, once the foundation of Japanese economic life, increasingly feel displaced by giant industry and department stores, and wonder if time is passing them by. To all of these, the New Religions say, "We can give you a modern and up-to-date way of getting the same spiritual values you left behind in the village. On top of that, we will give you friends, support, healing, and a

significant place in our group. We will take you seriously
and show that we care."

8. A fundamental message of all the New Religions is
that an individual makes his own world, his health or sickness, prosperity or poverty, joy or despair, through his
mental attitude. Through releasing the hidden potentials
of his true nature, as pure divine consciousness, he can
shape himself and shape his environment. The New Religions offer techniques for changing one's thoughts in a
constructive direction.

This mentalist philosophy doubtless has roots in Buddhism. Mahayana Buddhism, the Buddhism of Japan, says
that pure consciousness, the "Clear Light of the Void," is
the ultimate reality. The world of matter is always the
realm of multiplicity, partiality, and attachment, and
therefore is intimately connected with the delusion of not
seeing Absolute Reality as it is, even though the errors that
lead one to despair are rooted in false passions of the mind
and not in matter as such. Hence there is no final solace in
the world of appearance, and attachments to it are to be
shunned.

But starting from the same premise that consciousness is
prior to the outer visible world, the New Religions have
another approach, one far more optimistic in the ordinary
sense. They emphasize man's capacity to change conditions in the world by thinking bright, clear, positive
thoughts, and by releasing his own creative mental potential. Undoubtedly they are influenced by Western ideas of
progress, and philosophies of the power of positive thinking. For them, mind not only is deluded by matter but also
can control it. With a right attitude, there is nothing at all
wrong with living in the world of matter and rejoicing in it.

Thus, for Tenrikyo, the notion of reincarnation, which for the older Buddhism suggested a sad and bitter wheel of repetition from which one wanted to escape into nirvanic consciousness, is just like changing from one suit of clothes to another. On the average, successive lives will get better and better as the world moves toward its paradisal future. In a real sense, the New Religions are earth-centered, though not to the exclusion of God—for God or the Absolute is also concerned with the peoples of earth and their future.

The corollary of consciousness-is-all, though, is the individual's total responsibility through his thoughts for his situation and that of those around him. Here is where the darker side of human experience, the side touching guilt and anxiety, impinges upon the New Religions. If a person can make his world by the power of thought, it is no fault but his own if there is anything wrong with his world.

This is parallel to another Buddhist doctrine, that of karma, which teaches that the universe operates by inflexible cause and effect, in which mental and spiritual causes and effects interact thoroughly with material. In a world of karma, and of mentalism, nothing whatsoever in a person's life is really the result of mere accident, or just the way things are, or of circumstances beyond his control. Everything is the inevitable result of thoughts and actions in this life, or of an infinite chain of previous lives, coming to fruition in the present, just as by one's present he is making his future.

In the same vein, the rhetoric of the New Religions stresses that one cannot blame blind chance or poor social conditions or any other outside cause for lack of health or prosperity or happiness. It is always pressed home that it is really one's own fault, through thinking negative thoughts, and that the situation can be changed only within one's mental attitude.

In this, the effect of the modern malady of acute self-consciousness of separate, individual identity in the world is clear. In traditional Buddhism, suffering is the consequence of a vast cosmic web of karma impinging on the individual from out of billions of worlds and billions of aeons. The average individual could only modestly counteract the heavy weight of karma borne by his community, nation, and "conditioned reality" as a whole.

But in the New Religions, responsibility for good or ill in and around oneself falls directly on the thoughts of the individual here and now, in this life. The full burden, in all its potential for glory or terror, falls on each person in his aloneness. Not only can the modern, unlike the old peasant, effect in his own mind his weal and that of his family almost totally, but he can actively work to make the world a paradise, or he can defeat paradise—a presumption of power which would only have brought an indulgent smile to the lips of the Buddhist sage or serf of old.

This new responsibility is brought home pointedly and poignantly by something I have noticed in visiting American churches of the New Religions. I have been struck by the number of times I have heard sermons and classes in which citation was made of cases of parents who discovered that they themselves were responsible for the sicknesses of their children through unintentional negative thoughts.

This level of personal blame for all one's personal and family ills must go with a very high degree of self-consciousness. It suggests, as an aspect of modernization, the painful discovery of self with a new intensity, even though it may have Buddhist roots. It probably also has sources in the Confucian moral system which has long been very important in Japan, with its emphasis on right relationships between members of family and society. Confucianism imposes a very heavy burden of shame on those who behave contrary to right relationships: the unfilial son, the unparental parent, the disloyal subject. But the extent of half-conscious, subjective revolt against the old society is shown by the effective reversal of a cornerstone of traditional Confucian ethics. Tradition placed tremendous stress on the virtue of "filial piety," extended to include in fact unqualified fealty to one's feudal lord and the Emperor. Unbounded was the shame and guilt which fell upon one who failed even in thought, not to speak of actual deed, to give parents absolute obedience, reverence, and gratitude, regardless of any shortcomings on their part. Thus the declaration of innocence on the part of the child, and the transfer of personal guilt to the parent for the sufferings of the child, turns the former values upside down.

This all is a result of the radical self-discovery, and isolation, of the individual in the modern experience. It is connected to the fact that to enter one of the New Religions an individual must make a self-conscious, deliberate choice to leave the tradition and family-centered religion of his fathers to enter a new faith, requiring a high sense of his being a different person from others and living in a different world from the past. Decisions like this are made on a large scale only during the great turning points of history—the Hellenistic period, the Middle Ages in Japan, the era of the Reformation, the twentieth century.

Clearly, the psychological power of the New Religions rests in their ability to give one acute self-awareness and sense of responsibility, to raise powerful feelings of guilt, no doubt for the fruits of negative thoughts, and *then* to offer a way of resolving the guilt.

9. The New Religions put emphasis on physical healing. But physical healing seems to be increasingly deemphasized in them as time goes on. To some extent this is probably a response to medical criticism. It is also a result of increasing maturity of the mentalist philosophy, and a growing desire to apply it to larger problems than those of the physical body.

10. In communication, the New Religions tend to use the rhetoric of enthusiasm and testimony rather than argument. Sermons will be often a series of illustrative stories. The aesthetic—beauty, art, ritual, architecture—is a very important mode of expression too. They like to arouse conviction by means of the attractiveness of the human, the good, the beautiful, and the practical.

11. The final characteristic is that each has one *simple process* for releasing the inner power and thereby dispelling the guilt, finitude, and frustrations of a cramped life in which joyous mind does not reign supreme over circumstances. It may be chanting in Nichiren Shoshu, shinsokan meditation in Seicho-no-Ie, *oyashikiri* prayer in Perfect Liberty, Johrei in World Messianity, the daily sacred dance of Tenrikyo.

In conclusion, then, the New Religions have in common the founding by a charismatic, shamanistic individual, in an unstable social situation. They are partly influenced by a radicalization of the individual responsibility and mentalist motifs of the Buddhist and the Confucian backgrounds, partly by contact with the West. They have as common themes one God, a belief that Mind is all-powerful, hope of a New Age, belief in the possibility of commu-

nication with the spirit world, the establishing of a paradisal center in Japan, the formation of close-knit groups,
pilgrimage, healing emphasis, and focus on a single simple
action as the key to spiritual transformation and power.

VII

The New Religions started coming to America in force
in the 1960's. To be sure, some New Religions groups and
literature had been present before the war in the Japanese-
American community, but they had negligible impact outside that colony of gardeners, truck farmers, and traders in
an alien land whose lives were so brutally disrupted by the
great evacuation from the West Coast just after Pearl
Harbor.

But when the New Religions came back to America after
1945, most of them had new names and new features. They
reflected the great changes and new freedom in their
homeland. Nichiren Shoshu was revitalized by the Sokagakkai movement; the movement known as Hito no Michi
had become Perfect Liberty; Seicho-no-Ie was now ready
to establish American churches and training centers; and
Okada's movement, little known in America before the war,
had now adopted the universalist name World Messianity
and was ready to take its message everywhere. Only Tenrikyo, oldest of the major New Religions both in Japan and
in America, and the one most firmly planted in America in
the 1920's and 1930's, was relatively unchanged.

It was a transformed America too. Especially as America
moved into the decade of the '60s, it was an era of searching. Americans were searching into the further reaches of
the sea of consciousness. Above all, it was a search for intensity. Against the background of a culture that seemed
to many dehumanized, offering only competition, tract

houses at the end of freeways, and vicarious television reality, young people especially looked for ways to feel and know. God, or at least the way to God, was assumed to be found in intensity of feeling and acquaintance with the unconscious. To open up these channels of the soul many tried LSD, meditation, return to nature, and the Jesus movement.[5] It was presumed that spiritual reality was at the base of the self and could be opened up through the right insight or technique or style of life. But one needed a sure key to release it and let it gush up like a fountain.

The Japanese New Religions had the same basic assumption: Spiritual reality and power is something within that needs to be unleashed. Moreover, as we have seen, each of the New Religions offered a particular and suggestive insight as to the nature of this inner entrapped splendor, and a particular key, in the form of a simple practice, for releasing it. It is not surprising, then, that the Japanese New Religions and the American spiritual quest of the '60s were able to make contact.

The stage had already been set and the way cleared by the peculiar relationship of America and Japan in the late '40s and the '50s. During these years, millions of American servicemen and their families lived in Japan during the Occupation and, subsequently, were on duty at the many American military bases in Japan. For many, perhaps, the experience had no great effect on their values, but for some, like the Marine major, East and West would never be quite the same again.

All through history, military victory and the sending out of armies of occupation has affected the culture of the home country in the long run almost as much as that of the vanquished. The Roman legions left Italy to assure the security and economy of the ancient Republic, but they brought back with them not only grain and slaves, but strange gods—Mithra, Isis, Christ—and out of that melting pot a new world emerged. In our own day, the Zen of the 1950's and the Nichiren Shoshu and other New Religions of the 1960's have become attractive to Occidentals in America in large part through the conviction of returning servicemen and their Japanese wives.

The Japanese New Religions have had quite diverse fates in America. Each, in fact, has had three histories, one might say: a history in Japan, in the Japanese-American community, and among Americans of Occidental descent. In each, it has played a different role and had a different meaning to individuals.

In Japan, each is a revitalization of old shamanistic and Buddhist attitudes, together with enough syncretism to appear "modern." The New Religions represent a nativistic solution to the religious crisis of modernism, in contrast to imported solutions such as Marxism or Christianity.

Among Occidentals in America, on the other hand, the New Religions are part of the search for meaning in non-Western values. They appear as non-Western, exotic solutions. For some Western converts, this is part of their attractiveness: these adventurous spirits are sufficiently in reaction to the West that the exotic is appealing as an expansion of consciousness, or the vehicle for a new style of life. However much the New Religions may try to indigenize themselves in America, part of their attractiveness to some people will be always that they are never quite indigenous. These people want to acquire a new culture as well as a faith, or at least to taste another culture as they solve their religious problems. They like the fact that through the Japanese faith they can make Japanese friends, eat Japanese food, perhaps learn the Japanese language, and travel to Japan as honored pilgrims to the resplendent religious headquarters. Yet at the same time, the Japanese religion offers a faith which meets the spiritual quest for authentic subjectivity that overtook America in the '60s and '70s.

Among Japanese-Americans, in whose community they first took root in America, the New Religions play a role between these two poles. For many, they are certainly ties to home, family, and tradition. In contrast to the kind of Americans drawn to them, the Japanese in the New Religions in America are generally fairly traditional, conservative people—probably more "old country" on the average than Christian or nonreligious Japanese-Americans. They are Japanese who are close to Japan, and a rather traditional Japan at that, despite the religions' claims to modernity. Yet some Japanese younger people in the New Religions are eager for them to Americanize more—to use more English, sit in chairs more and on the floor less. To them, however, belonging to Tenrikyo or Perfect Liberty implies no more rebellion than belonging to the Methodist or the Presbyterian church among Occidentals; one gets a feeling the New Religions are even more socially respectable in the Japanese-American community, where of course there is no traditional village Shinto shrine, than in Japan. The churches are reasonably well organized and financed. Relationships to Occidental converts seem to produce no obvious, surface friction, despite the difference between the conservative, cautious Japanese-American constituency and the type of adventurous, "alienated" American who would likely enter them. But the situation is different in each New Religion, partly because each draws a quite different type of Occidental, as we shall see.

Indeed, the impact of each of these five upon the world of Occidental Americans has been diverse. Tenrikyo has won very few Occidental converts, but deserves a place in this book because of the special role it has as prototype of the New Religions and the especially interesting testimony of these few converts. Seicho-no-Ie also has few Occidental converts, but has a unique relationship to a new American religion, the Church of Religious Science. The Church of World Messianity has had a special role in the counter-culture, the Perfect Liberty faith in the rather different milieu of middle-class businessmen, many of them black. Finally, Nichiren Shoshu with its message of radiant joy through chanting has made a phenomenal impact among people of all ages, but especially youth.

It is now time to turn to the individual groups themselves.

2

Tenrikyo,
The Religion of Heavenly Wisdom

I

The tables before the four shrines were stacked high with neat piles of all sorts of fruits and vegetables, plus bottles of rice wine (*sake*) and one of Scotch whisky. The doors of the plain, cabinetlike shrines, constructed in the Shinto manner, stood open. Each revealed within a shining round metal mirror as a symbol of the presence of Spirit.

The shrine to the far right was dedicated to Miki Naka-yama, the nineteenth-century teacher who was the Foundress of the Tenrikyo faith, of which this church was the main American sanctuary. Before this shrine stood two striking red lanterns—for the Foundress wore red to show that she was no ordinary human being. The doors of the shrine to the Foundress, unlike the other three, remain open all the time, not just during services. This is because, just before her death at the age of ninety in 1887 (though she had been expected to live to be 115, the normal human age according to Tenrikyo), she said to her followers:

> *Sah! Sah!* I will step the ground level. *Sah! Sah!* With the portals opened, opened, level the whole ground. *Sah!* I will step out to level the ground. *Sah!* Shall I open the portals and level the ground; shall I close the portals and level the ground? [6]

Her listeners but poorly understood this saying, but said they would prefer to have the portals open. When shortly thereafter Miki Nakayama passed away (or, Tenrikyo people prefer to say, "hid her physical body"), the words were interpreted to mean that she had sacrificed the last twenty-five years of her life in order to leave the limitations of her body, universalize herself, and work on a spiritual plane throughout the world. In token of this, the doors of her red-lanterned shrine remain always open.

The central shrine of the four, and much the largest, is dedicated to the one God, called Oyagami ("God the Parent") by Tenrikyo. He is also called Tenri-O-no-Mikoto ("Divine Lord of Heavenly Wisdom") or Tsuki-Hi ("Moon-Sun"). This high deity it is who used Miki Nakayama, the Foundress, as his living earthly temple.

Then, to the left as one faces the central shrine is a shrine honoring the family of the Foundress, and to the far left, one commemorating the spirits of departed clergy and members of Tenrikyo, the religion of Heavenly Wisdom. This arrangement of shrines is not standardized, and most churches have only three. But all Tenrikyo churches (except the main temple in Tenri City) have a shrine to God the Parent, and a shrine to the Foundress, and one to the faithful departed.

The occasion was an enactment of Tenrikyo's chief ordinary service, held once a month on Sunday afternoon. Although it was a hot day in August, the church was comfortably filled with Tenrikyo faithful, most of them wearing black cloth jackets or kimonos with the name "Tenrikyo" and the designation of their local church or group written in Japanese or English on the lapels. The uniformed members tended to be older people; a sprinkling of younger Japanese and Occidental visitors were also present.

In the sanctuary of this church, which is in an old section of Los Angeles, a small, robed musical group sat with Oriental instruments. As the service opened they played the sort of music heard while offerings are being presented in Shinto shrines—shrill, reedy, unmelodious but very eldritch and mysterious flute tones with drum background. As they played, all the persons who wore the black Tenrikyo garments or kimonos came silently before the central shrine in groups, bowed, clapped four times, and returned to their places. Next, as the music continued, the attractive Shinto type of offering of green branches, set upright before the shrine, was presented by the principal priests.

Next the chief priest, wearing a formal black kimono, came before the altar to offer the saibun or prayer. Reading in Japanese from a scroll in a strained, chanting voice, he prayed to God the Parent for the church and the faith, for youth work, for the English-language work, and for the ultimate salvation of the world.

So far the service had followed a fundamentally Shinto model, though with important variations. Shinto worship begins with purification, proceeds to presentation of offerings and then to prayer, and finally to participation by all in the divine presence the rite has evoked. This last may take the form of sacred dance, which at once is a sublime offering of talent and beauty to deity and a manifestation of the splendor of the divine in our midst. But in the Tenrikyo service, the stress was different. There was nothing directed toward explicit purification, offering and prayer consumed a relatively brief amount of time, and the sacred dance was clearly the central event of the long liturgy.

New groups of performers came onto the sanctuary stage. The number of musicians and dancers was interesting. While teams changed three times, there were always eighteen in all. Three women musicians on the right played Japanese stringed instruments, considered feminine. In the center were six dancers, three men and three women. On the left six men played "masculine" instruments: a small hand drum, a large drum, gong, cymbals, clappers, and flute. Three more men were singers.

Of the three sections of the dances, the first was done seated, the second and third standing. But all put most emphasis on hand motions. The rhythm punctuated by the percussion instruments was strong. In most of the dances a brisk, gay stepping motion suggested a life of joy and confidence. The songs that the dances expressed are from the *Mikagura Uta,* or sacred dance songs, composed by Miki Nakayama to state lyrically the fundamentals of her theology. They tell of God's looking for the mankind he has created, seeing there is nothing which is really bad in the world, but only mental dust which has accumulated; and they recount of his teaching man to sweep it away. For, as the Tenrikyo scriptures put it, God says, "I created human beings because I wished to see them lead a joyous life."

The atmosphere of this service was informal, in the sense that most Asian worship from the Eastern Orthodox lands to Japan allows for a style of individuality in the ordinary devotee which Western European churches lack. In the West, everyone rises and sits, sings or prays, in unison as though at court or in a military drill. Characteristically, in the Tenrikyo service, while the precisely rehearsed dances were being performed, the congregation buzzed with whispers, individuals entered and left freely, or came to the front to put a gift in a large slotted offering box and say a prayer.

Yet the whole experience seemed to express the Tenrikyo idea of *yokigurashi*, the joyous happy life. The service is meant to be an expression of the joyful life, at once ordered and free, which God the Parent intends us to live. I am told that by participating in the performance as dancer or musician, as do most serious Tenrikyo members, one can really begin to get a feel of the *yokigurashi* life. The Tenrikyo dance is one way of expressing a theme that runs all through the New Religions, that life is an artistic expression. From one point of view, this means that life and worship must have that creative freedom which animates the true artist. But from another perspective, it means that the life which is joyful and spontaneous must also be structured and disciplined. To many Westerners this may seem a contradiction in terms. But a fundamental theme of both the New Religions and the older Oriental disciplines such as Zen is that a man must *learn* to be truly spontaneous, just as it takes an artist years of practice to draw lines that look easy and natural. Simply to follow the most superficial level of instincts and desires is not the joyful freedom of spontaneity, but its opposite. As Zen uses sitting to calm the outer shell of moods, feelings, and attractions, and thereby allow the inner well of joyful, creative spontaneity to arise, so Tenrikyo uses music and dance.

I got an impression of both the possibilities and the salutary difficulties of this method when I attended a daylong Tenrikyo training session. I had a chance to try several of the instruments, and found that, at least on the surface, they are fairly easy and very satisfying vehicles.

The heavy, captivating rhythm draws one, entranced, into a sense of vibrant participation mystique in the corporate performance as a whole, as he vigorously snaps the clappers or pounds a drum.

I also attended a training session in dance. Actually, it dealt not with one of the more advanced dances of the Sunday service but with the gestures and steps that accompany the first of the *Mikagura Uta:*

> Looking all over the world and through all ages,
>   I find no one who has understood My heart.
> So should it be, for I have never taught it before,
>   It is natural that you know nothing.
> This time I, God, revealing Myself to the fore,
>   Teach you all the truth in detail.[7]

This impressive poem is recited twice daily, with the gestures, in every Tenrikyo church and at each devout individual's private devotions. But for me, with my woeful muscular coordination, the hand signs were more than I could master in one day. Yet I could see that, when they came as easily as playing a familiar piece on the piano, or singing a childhood song, they could serve both as definer and carrier of the sacred moments of worship, preservatives against distraction, and expressions of the sentiments of the prayers. More than that, they help to unify many aspects of the self into one—body, motor energy, mind, emotions, words. Too often religious expression really pits these against each other, rather than allowing them to converge into a single statement.

II

In understanding the doctrine of Tenrikyo, as of any religion, the fundamental is understanding its concept of

God. We have seen that God is called Parent, Divine Lord of Heavenly Wisdom, and Moon-Sun. These terms bring to mind a God who is progenitor, who continually cares for man as a parent for his children, who has an intelligent plan for the creation, and who unites all opposites—Moon and Sun. (In Japanese mythology, the Moon is male and the Sun female.) In the Tenrikyo scripture, progressively revealed through the Foundress, the deity is first called God, then Moon-Sun, and finally Parent.

God the Parent unites polarities without being identified with his creation. In the language of the Tenrikyo scripture, the *Ofudesaki*, the universe is his body. The Tenrikyo God is unbounded, rising above the limitations of either a transcendent or a pantheistic concept. He works both immanently and in historical evolution. He is a God of that particularism which has always characterized Japanese religion, being manifest fully through one person in one place, but he is also said to embrace the whole universe without being limited by it. He is also spoken of as having ten *kami-na*, functions or aspects, which are like emanations in five male-female pairs.

The story of the creation of the world revealed through Miki Nakayama is very important to Tenrikyo. According to it, the world was originally an expanse of muddy waters. But God found this "unbearably tasteless," and determined to create human beings so that he could share their joy by seeing their *yokigurashi*. Searching through the waters, he called to himself eight creatures, that he might use them to make human beings. He called a fish, a white snake, a killer whale or orc, a tortoise, an eel, a flatfish, a black snake, and a globefish.

God put the orc into the fish; this became the seed of the first archetype of man, named Izanagi. He put the

turtle into the serpent; this became the seedbed or archetype of woman, and was named Izanami. At this point he
ate the other four creatures, with their consent; he tested
the mental quality or flavor of each for the qualities necessary for creation. The eel gave the functions of ingress and
egress; the flatfish, breathing; the black serpent, being
tough as a wire, childbirth; the globefish, the severing of
the embryo's connection at birth. Then God ate all the
mudfish of the ocean, and decided to use them as material
for human beings. Then God the Parent entered into Izanagi as the Moon and into Izanami as the Sun, and the
prototypes became the primal couple, and he taught them
how to procreate human beings.

Their first offspring were only half an inch tall, but later
generations gradually increased in height, passing through
all stages of existence: worm, bird, beast, and finally a
she-monkey, who gave birth to ten tiny humans. As they
grew, land and sea, heaven and earth, sun and moon began to shine and came to be discerned from out of dimness
of perception more and more. At last, man, five feet tall,
stood triumphantly on the land.

During the passage of these slow stages, for a first period
of nine hundred million and ninety thousand years, man
lived in the muddy waters. In the second period of six
thousand years, through the loving guidance of God the
Parent man's mind developed, and in the third period of
three thousand nine hundred and ninety-nine years man
learned reading and writing. Throughout this long period
God the Parent constantly guided and protected human
beings as they gradually matured physically, mentally, and
spiritually.

Even though man is essentially good in nature, and entitled to the wonderful goal of *yokigurashi*, the joyous life,

to which God is leading him, he has been ignorant of the story of his origins and has allowed his mind to be clouded by dust. *Yokigurashi* is a condition brought on by God the Parent, but man's responsibility for cleansing himself of the dust and his responsibility toward others do not cease. The relationship between God and man is a dynamic one, and *yokigurashi* is not a fixed state.

Man's ignorance of his origins has obscured for him an even more important fact, expressed in the words, "Things lent, things borrowed." Miki Nakayama said, "The human body is a thing lent, a thing borrowed; the mind alone is yours." The *Ofudesaki* tells us, "So long as you remain ignorant of the truth that you borrow your body from God, you can understand nothing at all."

All through the latter course of evolutionary development, the consciousnesses of men and women have been pursuing their own ways, determined by karmic cause and effect. Each body that a soul occupies for the span of a lifetime is only a thing lent to him for a time; after that life he will exchange the body for another as one would change a vesture. But the bodies have been given to us for good reasons: to amplify the possibilities of joy, and also to serve as instruments for God's warnings. The evils to which the flesh is heir are in this latter category. The *Ofudesaki* says: "Ponder over it deeply! There is nothing which should be called illness. They are all signposts or admonitions by God." And basically it is by the cleansing of the mind and spirit that poverty and illness are dispersed like dust from an unstained mirror through the providence of God.

Because of the doctrine of reincarnation, one has no future life except on this earth. This is an important point in Tenrikyo. There is no mystical assimilation to God the

Parent, no heaven or hell. One has no destiny except the wonderful joyous life here on earth for which man was made and placed on this earth. Man has no future life except incarnate in flesh in this universe. But life in body after body is everlasting and indeed splendid, and a glorious picture of the work that God the Parent will do to realize paradise for man on earth is unfolded.

In the garden of the home where the Foundress lived was a spot where, she taught, the creation of the world commenced. Here she constructed a temporary model of the central temple of the faith.

This place is now in the heart of the great mother-temple of Tenrikyo at Tenri City. In its very center is a pillar, called the *kanrodai,* fabricated of layers of wood, standing upright eight feet and two inches in an enclosed square recess in the floor. It thus marks the very spot of the ultimate origin. When all mankind is purified, the pillar will be made of stone and will be topped by a bowl of 2.4 gallons capacity, to be filled by a heavenly dew that God will rain down at the right time.

Around the pillar, on great festivals, ten dancers wearing masks represent the eight creatures God called together for the making of man, plus the leader of the faith and his wife, who represent the Creator as Sun and Moon. Normally invisible to the worshiping throngs as the temple is now constructed, they reenact the creation in a dance of sublime solemnity.

When God permits us to construct the *kanrodai* of stone, the joyous new age of the world will be ushered in. Men and women will live to the age of 115, then exchange their bodies for others in all peace, prosperity, and paradisal bliss on earth everlastingly. It will be a restoration and fulfillment at once of the pristine purity and purpose of creation ages ago. The importance of understanding the secrets, forgotten by most, of God's creation of man for Tenrikyo is told in these words of the *Ofudesaki*: "If you become aware of this origin in detail, there shall be no case in which you shall suffer from illness."

How shall we understand this account of man's origin, nature, and destiny? Miki Nakayama has given us a clue in the first chapter of the *Ofudesaki*.

> This is a world constructed on reason. So I will press upon you everything with the reason expressed in poetry.
>
> Though I say I press, I will never press by force or by mouth, but with the tip of My writing brush.
>
> It is all very well if you err in nothing. But should you err, I will warn you in poetry.
>
> It is a pity that when I warn you, things come to light. But it is inevitable, because any illness comes from one's own mind.
>
> What you are calling illness is not an ordinary one. Now I, God, am manifesting My anger.
>
> Hitherto also you had not yet obeyed what God had told you. So I was obliged to show it.
>
> The regret of God appearing in this illness is so severe that doctors and medicine are all powerless.
>
> Just this, never think that it is an ordinary illness! By all means I will drive it away with poetry.[8]

The very title of the scripture itself, *Ofudesaki*, means "the tip of the writing brush." If we see that Miki used simple words, such as "dust" and "dew," to direct thoughts in the oblique, suggestive, and profound way characteristic of poetry, the depths of the teaching can shine through. We can perceive a God in relation to men who have, solely by the blanketing dust upon their minds, brought illness and even bad crops upon themselves, alienating themselves from the joyous abundance rightly theirs. For the *Ofudesaki* says elsewhere:

> It is pitiful that you are of a mind that causes depressed crops. Therefore quickly become cheerful lest the crops be depressed!
>
> If you desire that the crops spring up vigorously, perform the *Kagura* [dance] and the *Teodori* [hand gestures]!
>
> Now set out to perform the *Teodori* in haste! Taking this as a signal, I will work marvels.
>
> This signal and the marvels have not yet been seen. But you will see them when the day comes.
>
> When the day comes and you understand what they are, whoever you may be, you will be all filled with admiration.[9]

To stimulate the joyous gestures that will reverse the untoward, unnecessary pain of the world caused by clogged minds, "an old woman of 72 years," as she here calls herself, admonishes by verse full of joyous hope God's angry rebukes, his searching the world for those who might remember, hitherto in vain. She calls up like a conjuring sybil the dances that will jog ancient interior memory and release anticipatory joy.

III

Who was this founding woman of Tenrikyo? She was born on June 2, 1798, of a peasant family near Nara in central Japan. The first seventy years of her life were lived in the waning years of the Tokugawa era, the two and a half centuries before the incursion of rapid modernization, when Japan was ruled by shoguns of the Tokugawa house. This regime imposed rigid, autocratic controls on society, which became more and more antiquated and burdensome as time went on. The economy deteriorated, and the first half of the nineteenth century saw frequent peasant revolts and cultic movements expressive of popular frustration. Characteristic were the so-called *Ee ja nai ka* dances. (The phrase means something like "It's all right," or "Anything goes.") Caught up in a dancing frenzy, hungry and desperate peasants would snake their way in a clapping, winding column uninvited through the homes of the prosperous and take whatever food or goods they wanted.

Miki Nakayama's early life was typical of that of a member of a farming family of her era. It was, despite the increasing dissolution, the last period of traditional Japanese culture, with its hierarchical social order and its folk religion full of magic and trance. Miki received a rudimentary education in a temple of Pure Land Buddhism. She was married young to a prosperous farmer and bore children. As a child and as a young adult, Miki's kindness and ability were widely noticed. But, as was the case with so many in those days of economic strain, the once-prosperous family grew poorer and poorer as the years went by.

In 1838, when she was forty-one, Miki's oldest son, Shuji, then seventeen, experienced a severe pain in the leg while he was working in the fields. Medical aid was of no avail, and the family decided to call an exorcist, named Ichibei, from a nearby village. Repeated visits turned out to be necessary. Shuji's relief after each spiritual treatment was only temporary; moreover, Miki's husband, Zembei, and Miki herself also developed ailments.

In the exorcising ritual of old Japan, it was customary for a female assistant, actually a medium, of the *yamabushi* to go into trance while holding two sacred staffs with paper hangings. It was believed she would then be

possessed by a god who would reveal the cause of the illness, and to whom the priest would deliver his incantations for its cure. On one of these occasions in the Nakayama family, Ichibei's usual assistant was not available,
and Miki was asked to act in her place. At first Miki's husband demurred, but Miki's own suffering, from a lower-
back ailment, became more intense, and he relented.

Miki performed a purification in cold water. Then,
seating herself, she took the two sacred staffs into her
hands. Suddenly, as Ichibei chanted, she fell into trance.
Her face altered to assume a look of tremendous majesty.
The priest reverently asked her what deity had descended
to possess her. The deity replied through Miki's lips: "I
am the True and Original God. Miki's mind and body will
be accepted by me as a Divine Shrine, and I desire to save
this world through this body." When Miki's husband hesi-
tated about Miki's accepting such an awesome vocation,
pleading that she was the mother of four children, the
deity answered, "If you refuse my desire, the Nakayama
family will completely cease to exist."

In the traditional Japanese manner, a long family council was convened to discuss this very unusual divine request. Miki remained in a trancelike state until, three days
later, the Nakayama family reluctantly decided that they
had no alternative but to concur with the desire of the
supreme God. Upon this decision, all members of the family found themselves completely healed of their illnesses,
and Miki herself was restored to her normal mental state.
But from then on, the Tenrikyo faith believes, the Foundress was God the Parent manifested on earth. Much later,
she interpreted the meaning of the charge she received
on that dramatic day in these words, cited before, which
open the *Ofudesaki* and are continually performed in the

Mikagura Uta, in which God himself tells what he was doing in and through Miki:

> Looking all over the world and through all ages, I find no one who has understood My heart.
> No wonder that you know nothing, for so far I have taught nothing to you.
> This time I, God, revealing Myself to the fore, teach you all the truth in detail.[10]

Miki's life changed radically. Serving continually as the Shrine of the High God, she presented an earthly appearance erratic and paradoxical. She reduced her family to the depths of poverty by giving away virtually all their possessions. Once the deity even told her to dismantle the house. She wandered about, like a divine fool, proclaiming the words of God. On several occasions, she came close to throwing herself into a pond or well, but an inner voice restrained her from taking her life at the last moment. In 1863 her husband died.

Yet out of all this distress came the teaching of the joyous life clouded only by dust. As the years went by, a few followers gathered around the quixotic, God-possessed women. They would dance through the streets, singing, "Hail, Tenri-O-no-Mikoto," and beating wooden clappers. But while the movement has as its social background the era of the *Ee ja nai ka* dances, probably Tenrikyo dance is more closely related to the role of folk dance in more traditional Japanese popular culture, such as the Obon dances. In any case, Tenrikyo dance was and is not frenzied or uncontrolled; if any of the same passions of protest and the crisis of modernity that created the *Ee ja nai ka* frenzy are also expressed in Tenrikyo, it is the genius of Miki Nakayama that she transmuted it into a positive and dignified religious expression. She created and taught all the movements of Tenrikyo dance, and every movement and gesture has a significance.

The movement coalesced. In 1863 a small shrine was built to Miki's god. Moreover, she was becoming widely known as a healer, especially in the matters of smallpox and safe delivery in childbirth. Through these doors, she said, would come the opening of universal salvation. In 1867 the movement was approved by the hereditary chief administrator of Shinto under the old regime, but the Meiji Restoration, the return (on paper) of direct imperial rule under the Emperor Meiji in the following year, made that action meaningless, for control of Shinto went directly to the central government.

The routinization of the Tenrikyo faith took place mostly in the Meiji period (1868–1912). This was a time of the westernization of Japanese society and government, but also of the increasing imposition of a nationalistic ideology in education and the regulation of religion. That caused new sorts of difficulties for an independent and strictly religious movement such as Tenrikyo.

Between 1866 and 1882, Miki wrote the poetic fundamental scriptures and taught the basic hand gestures (*teodori*) and dances. Another book with scriptural authority is the *Osashizu*, composed by Iburi Izo from 1887 to 1907, after the passing of the Foundress. The Master Iburi, as he is often called, succeeded Miki as leader of Tenrikyo and did much to effect its transition from an inchoate popular, charismatic enthusiasm to an organized church. The *Osashizu*, attributed to divine revelation, contains much more systematic and elaborate doctrinal statement than the earlier scriptures.

The early Tenrikyo movement attracted persecution,

first from Buddhist monks, then from the government. During the last decade of her life, Miki and her followers were harassed by the authorities, and Miki herself spent much time in jail. The basic reason for the persecution was that hers was not a recognized sect, her followers performed sacred dances in public view on the lawn of the Foundress' residence, an action considered provocative in an unauthorized and unregulated religious activity, and because she practiced what seemed to be "faith healing."

Miki would welcome her persecutors with smiles and blessings. On her return from prison she would be met by thousands of enthusiastic supporters, and say words like:

> Sah! Sah! Tsuki-Hi, God the Parent, having His being the world has its being; the world having its being, all things have their being; all things having their being, your bodies have their being; your bodies having their being, civil law has its being. Although there is law, the determination of the mind is of utmost importance. . . .
>
> Sah! Sah! Where there is sincerity, there shall be real providence. I suppose you don't know what is meant by the truth. True reality is fire, water, and wind.[11]

The faith grew rapidly in those days. In 1887, at the age of ninety, the Foundress passed away. After her death, the legal status of Tenrikyo was regularized by making it officially a Shinto sect (a status dropped after 1945), and the great sanctuary with the sacred pillar was built. It is believed that the Spirit of the Foundress dwells in the sanctuary to guide forever her faith and work for the salvation of the world; the temple is called "home" by all the faithful.

The vast and impressive sanctuary in classical Japanese architecture is now the focal point of Tenri City, near Nara. Within the sanctuary is a shrine to the Foundress, for whom meals are brought three times a day, and before whose altar priests are in constant attendance.

Outside the temple with its huge black *torii,* or gate, and its two and one half mile long graveled courtyard, Tenri City offers a fine university and library, a world-famous archaeological museum, and countless guesthouses, administrative offices, and classrooms. When I visited Tenri City in 1967 my wife and I were guests in a very spacious room, exquisitely decorated in greens and lavenders. We were afforded princely attention as we shared the life of that humming religious metropolis and were introduced to its faith and practice.

The extensive grounds are kept immaculate by the innumerable volunteer workers wearing the Tenrikyo jacket. They are donating labor, an important Tenrikyo religious duty. Most of them are members who come, as nearly all members do, to Tenri City for training sessions of three months' duration.

After receiving instruction, they will return as *yoboku,* missionaries, to spread the word of the joyous life. Classes, given in several languages, cover Tenrikyo doctrine, the dances, the scriptures, the life of the Foundress, and include hours for "living testimonials," in which students tell their own experiences in the faith.

Usually students at the center also attend a special series of lectures that will enable them to perform the rite called *Osazuke.* This is a healing prayer which is very precious to Tenrikyo. When it is conferred on the sick, the practitioner prays using hand gestures, then strokes the body of the patient three times. The performance is repeated thrice, making nine strokes in all.

The headquarters at Tenri City also confers the grant of safe childbirth, as it were in commemoration of the Foundress' first displays of charismatic power, which were in this area and that of healing smallpox. It is said that, if a mother requests it with complete faith, she will be guaranteed a safe and easy delivery by God. The grant must be received at Tenri City itself by the mother or a representative who is a member of the family. Several thousand of these grants are given each year, and have been responsible for many hopeful or thankful conversions.

IV

Tenrikyo first came to America only a few years after the passing of the Foundress, but the first ventures were not permanent. In July of 1896 a nineteen-year-old youth from Osaka named Sentaro Tamaki sailed for Canada, burning with passion to evangelize America. A number of other young Tenrikyo enthusiasts wanted to go with him, but were finally dissuaded by their families. Little is known of Tamaki's life in America, which seems to have been fruitless so far as propagating Tenrikyo is concerned. About 1914 he seems to have been living in Los Angeles, but he has not been heard of since that time. An early mission in England, this one officially sponsored and financed by the church, lasted only from 1910 to 1919 even though it was supported by an English merchant, T. A. Lose, who had become converted to Tenrikyo in Japan, and produced a very small number of other Occidental converts. Missions to other parts of East Asia were more successful.

In 1926 the church established a foreign-language school to prepare for overseas work in earnest. This school in time became Tenri University. However, outside of East Asia successful work was almost entirely limited to Japanese immigrants. The first U.S. church was founded in San Francisco in 1927. The following year other churches were established by missionaries in Portland (Oregon), Seattle, Sacramento, Los Angeles, and Salt Lake City. Within a few years Tenrikyo churches flourished in scores of cities and towns in the western part of the United States and in Hawaii, wherever sizable Japanese populations existed. The work also spread to Brazil about the same time. In 1933 the Shimbashira, head of the faith and descendant of the Foundress, came to America on a tour in which he visited all the churches in person. A permanent U.S. Mission Headquarters was established in Los Angeles in 1934.

In 1974 there were two and half to three million adherents throughout the world—this number may be compared to the figure of two million given for ten years after the death of the Foundress. The U.S. membership was about two thousand, located in some sixty churches and missions. Five hundred and fifty of the U.S. members are *yoboku*, lay missionaries who have completed the three-month training course at Tenri City and can give *Osazuke*. About 30 percent of the membership is under thirty. Over 99 percent is Japanese.

The relative lack of Occidental converts is undoubtedly due to the fact that the teaching and the mode of worship, more than in the case of the other New Religions, seem impenetrably alien and Oriental to most Westerners—the mysterious instruments and dance, the myth of creation and salvation which sounds so strange to Western ears.

Paradoxically, though, another reason is the striking parallels between Tenrikyo and Christianity. There is the familiar personal God, expressing both parental love and rebuking anger toward man, who creates the world, makes man the special crown of his creation, comes to him in a single individual whose sacrificial love and sufferings and words are a divine drama of communication, and promises a paradisal new earth.

When one listens to Tenrikyo theologians discuss such things as exactly in what sense the Foundress was human and in what divine, or how her sufferings accomplished man's salvation, or the precise meaning of the *Ofudesaki*'s inspiration, one has a strange feeling he could but change the terms and be listening to a group of fairly conservative Christian theologians—though it is hard to imagine Christ as a woman, or living less than a hundred years ago. But the Eastern religions successful in the West today are those most different from the Judeo-Christian tradition in concept of God, man, and the spiritual path, since they meet needs many people feel, but for which there are no other evident recourses here. A person inclined toward the kind of religion that Tenrikyo appears to be would in most cases probably be well enough satisfied with Judaism or Christianity.

Yet a handful of Westerners have found Tenrikyo most satisfying to their religious desires. They seem to be people who were strongly alienated from Christianity for various reasons, yet not the sort of persons drawn toward mysticism and meditation, as many temperamentally are not. As far as I have been able to learn, Americans of Occidental ancestry have joined Tenrikyo only since the war. In some cases they are people who had considerable military or business experience in Japan, and acquired a love for the Japanese culture and people, of which Tenrikyo consciously or unconsciously became a symbol. The beauty of the faith's ritual expression in dance, and the brilliance of Tenri City, became for them the best of Japan.

Of course, Tenrikyo doctrine had a powerful appeal too.

Western converts have penetrated far enough into it to see that the apparent similarities between Christianity and Tenrikyo go only so far, and that at base the two religions entertain quite dissimilar concepts of the nature of God and man. The parenthood of the Tenrikyo God is not understood in Father terms, but as equally Moon and Sun, Father and Mother. Everlasting reincarnation on this earth rather than final judgment after one lifetime greatly reduces the quality of anxious seriousness in the faith, as does the idea that man is not radically "fallen" and in rebellion against God, but basically good even though his mind, the source of all weal or ill, is obscured by dust. The emphasis on man's purpose being just to live a joyous life here on earth, and the main expression being non-verbal music and dance, sets a different tone—a lighter, gayer, more aesthetic and indirect tone—than much of Christianity, with its preaching, repentance, and stress on decision for or against Christ. Set down on paper, the two faiths probably look more alike than they are in experience.

An article by one Western convert, Walter Pennington, gives his reasons for adhering to Tenrikyo.[12] He says that a fundamental search of his has been for the secret of having a passion for right living. Note the subtle but all-significant nuance in this phrasing: he desired not just to know how to live rightly, but to know how to *desire* to live rightly, indeed, to know how to have a *passion* for right living. In this quest, he found that although man can perhaps lead a good life as a nonreligious humanist, he does not sustain the fire of a passion for right living without inspiration from a source higher than the unheroic human level. What seemed to embody better than anything else the kind of inspiration Mr. Pennington was looking for was the happy, affirmative, yet passionate Tenrikyo ideal of *yokigurashi*—the joyous life lived on earth as man's God-promised destiny. He liked the fact that Tenrikyo does not create despisers of the world, that it finds ennobling all essential work no matter how lowly, and does not dwell on sin but dwells on affirmation. He also likes its attitude toward the religious quest and toward other religions, which he found to be open, tolerant, and mature.

Another Westerner, Forest E. Barber, begins with an account of his disillusionment with Christianity.[13] It is a familiar story: a boy in a conservative Midwestern town who accepted what he was taught in church until he began reading books on science and history in public libraries and who finally went into reaction against his background and came to hold the rather extreme opinion that the history of Christianity is one of little more than obscurantism and violence. He then searched the world trying to find a faith he could accept.

Mr. Barber did not hear of Tenrikyo until he read an article in *Fate* magazine about the Foundress and Tenri City. Something about that account infatuated him, and he tracked down all the information he could on this Japanese faith. In time he visited an American Tenrikyo church, where he was received with great warmth and hospitality. The divine beauty of the dancing worship stirred him deeply. Soon he was teaching a Tenrikyo Sunday school class, and was on his way to Japan to take the course at Tenri City.

I interviewed another American member of Tenrikyo, George Blesch, who has been to Tenri City twice and who joined two years before the 1972 interview. He is leader of a Tenrikyo mission in Cupertino, California.

Mr. Blesch was raised a Lutheran, but dropped out of active church participation while in college, feeling that from his own point of view there was too great a divergence between what was taught by the church and the way the church members lived. He spent five years, 1953–1958, in Japan as an engineer with an American corporation. During this period he married a Japanese girl. He was unaware of Tenrikyo, however, until after he returned to the United States.

In 1966 his wife's father was killed in an automobile accident. His wife returned to Japan for the funeral and the settlement of the estate. Her mother had quietly been a member of Tenrikyo, it turned out, for fifteen years. While in Japan on this sad occasion, Mr. Blesch's wife also joined Tenrikyo. This was a result of the strength which Tenrikyo had given her mother, and her attitude toward events during that time of difficulty. She understood death in the Tenrikyo manner to be just a changing of garments, and she did not join with other relatives in petty squabbling over the estate.

Mr. Blesch's interest in Tenrikyo also stems from that time. His wife practiced Tenrikyo faithfully, and he noticed a marked change in her attitude. A few years later he himself joined the faith.

When I asked Mr. Blesch what was most attractive to him about Tenrikyo, he seemed to have trouble answering, so many things came to mind. First, though, he mentioned that Tenrikyo teaches there is a stated *objective* to life. It has an answer to the question, Why are we here? The answer is to live a joyous life on this earth.

Second, he said that because of his engineering training, he wants a teaching that is satisfying from a philosophical and logical point of view. In Tenrikyo, the tenets all hold together. I mentioned that some Westerners find the creation story bizarre and unscientific. This seemed to surprise him. He said that to him it was really similar to Darwin in its evolutionary aspect, together with having a concept of purpose and growth. The fundamental thing of importance in the story of creation is what God the Parent is telling us in it. We may not be able to explain all the mechanical details scientifically, but that is secondary to the sense of meaning in life that it imparts.

He added also that he enjoys the Tenrikyo service. In one's first experience, it may seem rather long and boring, but after one comes to some understanding of its meaning and takes part at times in the performance, he finds that the time seems to get shorter. The dance as *the* way of salvation makes us joyous and melts us into the divine heart. The main theme of the service is a *unity* of body, heart, and mind, and of doing things in unison with others.

He has also been impressed with the fact that Tenrikyo followers live what they preach. Perhaps not quite as much here as at Tenri City, but then Tenri City is an ideal, a life all Tenrikyo twenty-four hours a day. It is, indeed, a problem to make the transition back from Tenri City to the "outside world," but that is a transition which has to be made. In any case, though, he stressed that the teaching and practice of Tenrikyo is not a Sunday-only matter. One does the first section of the *Mikagura Uta* service every morning and evening, and anyone can do it.

Our discussion then went back to the creation story. Mr. Blesch emphasized that, because of the way God the Parent created mankind, we are all from the same source; we are all brothers and sisters here together to live the joyous life. This joy is attainable only if we *act* as though we were brothers and sisters. Coupled with it is the idea that material things are not really things that belong to us —when we lose them, it is just a loan returned.

The Tenrikyo teaching about reincarnation, too, is distinctive. It is quite different from the Hindu and Buddhist concepts, in which reincarnation is a fact, but a gloomy one, an enslavement on an everlasting wheel from which we should want to escape into nirvana. But in Tenrikyo, we *want* to return to this earth. There is no life for us anywhere else. We can't think in terms of leaving this earth, but we can think in terms of helping to make it better.

This led to a consideration of Tenrikyo ethical principles. Tenrikyo has been criticized for having no thoroughgoing rules in matters of morals and ethics. For Mr. Blesch, one of its great virtues is that its moral teachings are not highly codified. Because of this, there is more individual responsibility. There is, in fact, just one basic principle: Do any action that will make another person happy. We are here to live a joyous life and help others live a joyous life. There are no strict prohibitions on such matters as diet, drinking, and smoking. The scriptures, such as the *Ofudesaki*, give a certain tone and inspiration, but are general rather than specific. In these and all other respects, if something would make another person unhappy, don't do it; whatever would make another happy, do. The obligation to discern which is which is up to you. Bear in mind also, he went on, the fact that your body is a thing lent; the obligation does not include saving yourself or your own happiness at the cost of another. But keep your mind happy; you *do* own your soul-mind which passes through many bodies.

We commented on the fact that, unlike some Eastern religions, Tenrikyo does not put a lot of stress on medita-

tion. But there is a place for introspection in determining
what God has asked us to do in a situation.

He said that Tenrikyo has only an *apparent* similarity
to Western religion. There is not as much similarity as
seems on the surface. Reincarnation is certainly one difference. Monotheism they both have in common, but the
Tenrikyo God has a different character, being both male
and female. For real unity we need a uniting of these two,
like the union of fire and water which makes water boil.

God, in short, is simply *Parent,* and one of endless love
and wisdom. Our sufferings are looked upon not as divine
punishment but as divine guidance. They may derive from
previous incarnations or present acts, but they are meant
to cause us to fall back into introspection until we realize
what God is trying to tell us through them.

Death, Mr. Blesch added, is not a thing to be afraid of
at all. One just gives up one body, and then he will be
back. He is not conscious during the interval in between.
There is no end to the process of life after life, though
there was a beginning—the creation. For, finally, it must
be remembered that this earth developed *with* man. Our
minds have been on this earth, in fish and animals, all the
way through evolution. Man was in principle created first.
Now we are completed physically, except for ills we bring
upon ourselves, but our minds will go on evolving to un-
dreamed-of powers and joys. In all of this, I thought, Tenrikyo has something in common not only with Darwin but
also with the philosophy of Teilhard de Chardin.

V

Westerners have no position of leadership in American
Tenrikyo except as heads of fellowships or missionary centers. One joins Tenrikyo simply by attending a church reg-

ularly; the real initiation is going to Tenri City to take the training course and becoming a *yoboku,* or missionary, and receiving authority to confer *Osazuke.*

Most Japanese-American members of Tenrikyo are second- and third-generation descendants of Japanese immigrants. Church organization follows a rather conventional pattern, with men's organizations, women's organizations, young peoples groups, Sunday schools, and so forth. In addition, a Tenrikyo church typically will have a Japanese culture association. The Los Angeles church has a fine judo hall where classes are given in that ancient sport, and it has an excellent library.

Each church has a board of directors appointed by the minister to administer the property. The ministers, often eldest sons of ministers, volunteer for this work and are ratified in office by the headquarters in Japan.

Close relationships with Tenri City are maintained. The Tenrikyo mission in America has an admirable program of sponsoring student exchanges, sending American students to study at Tenri University, and sponsoring Japanese students in America. Pilgrimages that the faithful make "home" to the main church, the *Ojiba,* are of course important. There is no special organization for Occidental members, most of whom seem to have a rather individualistic relation to the church. There is, however, an English presentation of doctrine during services or afterward.

I once attended a discussion of Tenrikyo teachings at an American training seminar. As is often the case, talk turned to the exact nature of God's revelation in Miki Nakayama. On the blackboard the basic facts were outlined with a typical Japanese clarity about such concrete information: the person, Miki Nakayama; the place, the *Ojiba* (site of the present main sanctuary in Japan); the time, October 16, 1838, 900,999,999 years after the creation. Her mind, the minister said, was taken over by God the Parent. God the Parent's mind replaced Miki's mind, although she was otherwise "normal."

The present theory, he said, is that the remaining fifty years of the Foundress' life were a *continuous* revelation, day and night. What about when she wanted to commit suicide in a well or pond? She, as God, was *showing* people the struggle of being in that position. Yet she *did* suffer, and God's being in her means more because of that.

Tenrikyo people love to discuss their doctrine, and also to discuss and analyze in detail the performance of their highly liturgical religion. Discussion turned to the great dance of creation enacted around the pillar at "home." We talked about the positioning of the dancers, the meaning of the white strings that connect some but not all of the performers, and why the dance cannot be seen. The minister explained that it is not meant to be secret, but that it cannot be seen because of the way the sanctuary is constructed. The names of the sea animals—for example, whether it is a killer whale or orc—is not important; only their function is important.

I was interested in the sorts of questions put by Japanese-American and Occidental persons present at this discussion. Some of the Japanese-Americans clearly represented a new generation committed to the faith, yet impatient in some ways with its present structure. They asked such things as why the worship had to be so Shinto-like when the church has long since renounced all ties to Shinto, why the clergy wear such peculiar gowns, why training standards for missionaries are not higher, why they have to sit on the floor in many church situations in the Japanese manner, why the English translations are not better. These are the sorts of questions which critical, slightly cynical Americans, with little sense of sacred mystery and tradition, might ask.

All the clergy could do was point out that most of these things—vestments, Shinto and other old-country customs —were not part of the original revelation, but just traditions and adaptations. They could be changed and probably would be, owing to the presence of overseas churches, especially the large Korean church which is understandably highly antithetical to anything Japanese and especially anything Shinto. But the headquarters is cumbrous and moves slowly.

Regarding the hiddenness of the sacred dance of creation, a question mentioned earlier, as a historian of religion I myself was able to throw in an idea. I pointed out that in Japan, unlike the West, what is most sacred is most hidden. The sacred object in a Shinto shrine which represents the deity may be kept concealed in an inner chamber entered only at great festivals, and then just by the priest. Some famous Buddhist images are shown only one day a year. The more holy something is, the more it is to be veiled, obscured, just alluded to or pointed toward. It may be that in the West we feel there should be "no secrets" in religion, and place the sacred object, Bible or Sacrament, on the high altar, in full view; but the difference between this approach and Japanese reticence should be considered a matter of cultural attitude, not a moral issue. In the tendency of younger people to raise characteristically Western lines of criticism, one could sense the degree of generational psychological shift in these children of immigrants, and the problem it will raise for the church.

Caucasian Westerners, on the other hand, had different kinds of problems. Westerners in Eastern religions will be people perhaps more in love with Eastern attitudes than they are with Western, perhaps more than many Eastern people themselves are today.

One Westerner present was a fiftyish man with a ragged gray-black beard, bib overalls corded into pantaloons around his ankles, and a sharp-eyed, white-haired wife dressed in an equally unorthodox lavender gown. They were quite in contrast to the conservative Japanese, all cleanshaven and wearing neat sport shirts and even ties. This man talked of the Ancient Wisdom and the tendency of all religions to decline from the purity of the original teaching, and asked if Tenrikyo would keep itself pure and at the same time not get "dogmatic and orthodox."

This meeting ended with a Tenrikyo service in the church. Five clergy entered the sanctuary before the four shrines wearing black gowns with ornate silver-white cording around the collar and waist. On their heads were elaborate black caps, pointed and with a tassel hanging down the back. They started chanting to the beat of drums and clappers and cymbals as they sat in a row before the main shrine. The percussion rose to a thrilling climax suggesting the mighty dancelike activity of deity. The congregation recited the *Mikagura Uta* with hand gestures, mystically becoming God the Parent searching the world for any who remembered, walking out briskly into saving action, and descending on his chosen vessel. Then, after bowing and clapping, all exited, to make their way out into the American streets.

READING SELECTION

The following passage, from the Ofudesaki *of Miki Nakayama, suggests the sense of new divine initiative, sur-*

prise, and wonder that is so much a part of the Tenrikyo experience.

Perhaps you may wonder what it means for Me to go out. Understand that it means that I, Tsukihi, will go out to meet you!

Today the time is sufficiently pressing. There is no knowing what kinds of ways will appear.

Determine your mind firmly, all of you of the whole world! At any moment, I, Tsukihi, will go out to take you away.

Today I will begin to tell you a remarkable thing. No one knows what kinds of things I am going to say.

In the world everyone everywhere is the same. People prepare to marry off their children.

However carefully you might have prepared, no one can know how it shall turn out thereafter.

What intention I, Tsukihi, may have; there is no one who knows the course of the way.

In the future you may see a dream which you have never expected. Thence everything shall be changed, and you shall become cheerful.

There is no knowing what a remarkable dream you may see. Taking it as a signal, begin to perform the Service!

—*Ofudesaki: The Tip of the Divine Writing Brush* (Tenri, Japan: The Headquarters of Tenrikyo Church, preliminary edition, 1971), XVI:20–28, pp. 441–443.

3

Nichiren Shoshu of America

I

I once attended a Nichiren Shoshu chapter meeting in a modest one-story frame house in a suburban city. The living room of this bungalow had been converted into a shrine room. At the end opposite the door rested a dark-brown cabinetlike box, with the doors open to reveal a rectangular sheet of paper crowded with Japanese characters. Incense hung in the air. When I arrived at seven in the evening, four or five young people were already seated on the floor, chanting. Others kept coming in, until within half an hour thirty-five or forty were present. At first the meeting was rather informal. People whispered, went out to take phone calls, greeted friends enthusiastically—but as the crowd gathered in, it also settled down.

The chant was recited very fast. There was an accompanying dry rustle from the Buddhist rosary of 108 beads, shaped roughly like a human form, with a central loop and five attached limbs. Words were pronounced in the manner of Japanese monks, with consonants swallowed, leaving only a bouncing series of vowels. The fast chanting left a singing resonance in the air, like all words and no words. Actually, the chant was the syllables *"Nam Myoho Renge Kyo."*

Eventually, after some forty-five minutes, the first part of the evening ended as the leader sounded a bell three times. That marked the transition to Gongyo, the recitation of a part of an ancient Buddhist scripture, the Lotus Sutra. It was read in unison with racing speed, in the ancient Chinese-Japanese pronunciation of the Sanskrit original. In this group reading, it is the sound rather than the meaning that counts. Gongyo sounded like the combined hum and rhythm of an express train clicking along the rails. One could not help tapping or swaying to its vibrations. It was an exotic sound: closing my eyes, I could see ancient curved-roofed monasteries, reflected in lotus ponds or banked with Himalayan snows.

A few minutes later, though, I was definitely back in the twentieth century and in America. Six or seven vivacious girls got up and led several Nichiren Shoshu songs in cheerleader fashion. The assembly, mostly young, well-fed and well-scrubbed Caucasians dressed in fashionable informality but not to extreme, leaned back and applauded vigorously.

Visitors were introduced. Then, for the sake of the visitors, several members of the chapter gave explanations. They always spoke of Nichiren Shoshu as "this philosophy," not "this religion," although one could hardly imagine any phenomenon that would *look* more "religious" to the outsider than bowing before an Eastern altar, rubbing rosaries, and chanting words of adoration in an ancient tongue.

However, the speakers said that Nichiren Shoshu is "True Buddhism," a philosophy going back three thousand years to Sakyamuni Buddha,[14] but fulfilled in Nichiren in the thirteenth century A.D. He was the first to chant "*Nam*

Myoho Renge Kyo." But the philosophy did not become freely available to everyone until after the war, because, we were told, the government in Japan always suppressed it since it made people happy, and they found people easier to control if they were not happy. The object of Nichiren Shoshu, it was said, is world peace. But world peace had to start from within: "You can go on peace marches, but if you're messed up inside, argue with your wife and so on, it doesn't do much good." Nichiren Shoshu, it was further said, is for *everybody*, "whether you're smart or dumb."

A large sign on the wall beside the altar read "30 Days to Sho-Hondo." That alluded to the number of days until the great dedication service for the new temple at the world Nichiren Shoshu headquarters at the foot of Mt. Fuji. Shortly afterward, this dedication and the building itself, with its extraordinary architecture, received world publicity. A spokesman at the meeting I was attending said the reason for the sign was that many people had promised to do something—chant so many times, for example—before the date the new Sho-Hondo, or head temple, opened. The new temple houses the original Gohonzon made by Nichiren. The Gohonzon is the rectangular white sheet of paper inscribed with characters toward which the chanting was directed. All the Gohonzons used in the homes and meeting places of Nichiren Shoshu people are transcriptions of this original Gohonzon, which, tradition says, was made by Nichiren himself in the Middle Ages. It is the supreme object of worship in Nichiren Shoshu, and stories are told of its great efficacy. One speaker that evening said it is a marvelous thing that people who have gone to it in Japan have come back with hopes fulfilled and wishes granted. (On October 7, 1972, this original Gohonzon was solemnly moved from the old temple to the vast and gleaming new sanctuary. Some three thousand overseas visitors were present, many from Nichiren Shoshu of America. The ceremony culminated with chanting and Gongyo, together with more esoteric rites performed only by priests of the Nichiren Shoshu denomination of Buddhism.)

It was now time for testimonies. In their eagerness to speak, attenders did not merely raise their hands but threw them into the air, almost jumping up and down with excitement. A tall brunette, radiant with health, youth, and beauty, told that before she started chanting two years before, she had been "down," but now she was happy. She had a problem, though: too much to do. She had to ride her horse, go to school, work in her father's restaurant, and attend Nichiren Shoshu meetings. Her father had tried to make it hard for her to attend meetings and chant. But she had been able, thanks to chanting, to work it all out, and she had even gotten into a ceramics class at school that she had wanted to take but that was overenrolled.

Another girl said that she had been chanting for her mother's happiness; her mother, she said, had been going through a hard period for the past year. The daughter was also tired of their house, in which they had lived since she was six. The very day after she started chanting for a new house, her mother put it up for sale, and it sold quickly. Another thing, this girl said, she had just gotten a thousand dollars "in an incredible way, and needed the money."

A young man, a musician, told of obtaining a good job and getting his guitar fixed free by the help of Nichiren Shoshu members.

All the speakers related what had happened to them

with shining faces, if sometimes with stumbling words, and all said that the spiritual benefits of Nichiren Shoshu are the greatest, that the material good luck, large or small, which seemed to accompany the onset of chanting was secondary to the inner change it had made in them. This was evident from the tone and intensity of the testimonies. For many people, improvement in material wellbeing, or on the level of finding more satisfying friends, work, and self-image, is easier to talk about than the purely inner change which lies behind them; but, as Nichiren Shoshu says, the inner change is the real source of the outer.

One boy said that he had been "stoned" quite a bit of the time before he began chanting. He had taken mostly humanities courses in college and had gone through them in a dreamy way. Then the day came when he had to get a job. At first, his attitude toward the "straight" business world was so negative that he refused even to wear a suit all day when he went out looking for work. He just took one with him, put it on before he went into a firm, and took it off when he came out. Eventually, he did find a place in an accountant's office. He said that it was hard for him to accept the business world with its people and values, but with the help of chanting it became easier; that was perhaps evident from his short hair and clean-shaven face.

A smiling, wild-haired young man reported that at first what had repelled him about Nichiren Shoshu was the claim that it was for everyone, smart or dumb. He was an elitist, he said. Most people were just in his way; anything for everyone was not for him. He wanted a way that only he and maybe two or three other people could follow. But finally friends persuaded him to try chanting.

You can, he said, just try chanting on a test basis, since it's scientific, based on cause and effect. What amazed him was its effect on his spiritual life. He had to mention this, since so many people tend to talk just about material benefits.

True, he got money by chanting, but went through it fast. So he found a job through another Nichiren Shoshu member as a telephone solicitor selling books. Even though he woke up housewives in the middle of the morning with his pitch, he was such a good talker (evident in his present discourse!) that he had fascinating conversations, due to the ebullient power of chanting, and had moved up to become top salesman. He was, he added, no longer an elitist; world peace has to come through something for everyone.

The leader, a clean-shaven, short-haired, portly young man wearing a white shirt and tie, ended the testimonies. He said that he too had been argumentative and had rebelled against his parents and his background. The audience laughed as he added, "Sometimes with good cause." But rebellion wasn't the solution. We need to change inside. He mentioned a Nichiren Shoshu principle, *esho funi*, inner and outer are not two things, indicating that one's environment reflects oneself, what one is inside. Chanting can clean you out, he went on, and make you a new person. Material benefits come with being a new person, but the real point is spiritual. Try it for a hundred days, he pleaded . . .

He announced that a Gongyo class would be held afterward. Gongyo, the chanting of selections from the Lotus Sutra, is hard but necessary, he explained. It should be done every morning and evening, along with chanting. He couldn't clarify, he said, what the chant is, why it works, or what Buddhism is. But he knows, he added with a radiant smile, what effect it has on him.

He then talked about procedures for "solicitation," inviting others to try Nichiren Shoshu, and about a "marathon" scheduled for the coming weekend for selling the Nichiren Shoshu paper, the *World Tribune*.

II

This is the atmosphere of Nichiren Shoshu, the Japanese religion that has been by far the most effective in winning Occidental adherents. The only objective criterion for "joining" Nichiren Shoshu is to have a Gohonzon—the altarpiece with the characters on it—installed in one's home. Following the usual Japanese practice, Nichiren Shoshu considers that when a Gohonzon is placed in a home, all immediate members of the household should be counted as within the orbit of the faith. For this reason, exact statistics are hard to determine, and most Nichiren Shoshu people give the impression of not really caring how many adherents could be counted by external means. I have seen estimates of the number of Nichiren Shoshu people in America ranging from 100,000 to 300,000 published in the media in the early 1970's. Twenty million adherents are claimed worldwide, most of them being in Japan.

The important thing is that Nichiren Shoshu is making an impact. All sorts of people are in Nichiren Shoshu, and have found it to have changed them. Countless cases are described in the *World Tribune*. A young man was interested in music but was able to get a job only as a busboy. He heard about Nichiren Shoshu and the *"Nam Myoho Renge Kyo."* When he got into the organization, he started playing in a Nichiren Shoshu brass band and developed his talents. Later he found a job as a repairer of musical instruments, owing to some breaks he attributed to chanting. Another young man broke into film in much the same way, and says he got his best idea, a cartoon of a boy whose kite turns into a dragon, while chanting! Over and over again, we see people for whom a clogged-up life undergoes a breakthrough to new levels of achievement, and chanting is seen in a key relationship to the process. This is what Nichiren Shoshu calls "true humanism," and to them it is real Buddhism in action.

It is at the great annual conventions that the real dynamic of Nichiren Shoshu comes out. These meetings have drawn as many as twenty thousand people. They are splendid occasions, full of fun and festivity. There are great parades with all sorts of fantastic motifs in bands and floats, programs combining music with chanting and addresses, sight-seeing tours, and euphoric fellowship. One gets a taste of the combination of religion with travel and celebration, exemplified in Chaucer's pilgrims, carnival in Brazil, holi in India. It is an old and joyous theme in human culture, but, except for Mardi Gras in New Orleans, is too much lost in modern America. The convention signifies that Nichiren Shoshu is trying to bring back to us, preoccupied as we are with religion as a matter of the anguished, guilty, or merely ethical individual soul, the idea that religion should, after all, give man his most effervescent and most communal hours, and that these should go together in what has anciently been religion's high points, the pilgrimage and the festival. Like a holiday of old, these conventions are gaudy, gay, tiring, and immensely fun. Far removed from the usual staid church council, or the ordinary secular convention, they are at once innocent, sacred, and human. They bring people together in charter flights to the greatest halls available in major cities. Delegates wear identical clothes, parade together, share their talents, sing Nichiren Shoshu songs, cheer, worship. Countless pageants put across Nichiren Shoshu teachings through Japanese, African, or outer space themes.

Even limited contact with Nichiren Shoshu followers makes it evident that the movement is doing a mighty task in the resocialization of people who were formerly alienated, lost in meaninglessness, or just "mixed up," giving them a positive self-image and an acceptance of American society. They have come to have an affirmative attitude toward work, the capitalistic system, neatness, respect for parents, the American past.

It may seem strange that this sort of reconciliation should come about through the instrumentality of a religious practice of such utterly non-American cultural background. Yet such has been the case. Nichiren Shoshu reinforces this process by encouraging neatness, external conventionality, and responsibility. It also seems more and more to be encouraging a positive attitude toward America. The American flag is prominently displayed at its major centers. At recent conventions, two-hour pageants on American history have had a leading place.

For Nichiren Shoshu, all of this is tied to the central experience: that its practice of chanting is a liberating, releasing, and identity-giving thing. The practice cleans out everything within the person which separates him from his environment and his own true nature and which blocks creativity. It makes him, like a Buddhist bodhisattva, able to act *spontaneously* from out of the ground of his being. Nichiren Shoshu perceives that for an American in America (the same would be true of a Japanese in Japan, or a person of any other culture in his homeland) to feel out of harmony with his family, his country, and its traditions would essentially represent a blockage, a one-sided angle of vision based on partiality of perception and emotion-tinged attachments to pet egotistic attitudes. All this falls short of Buddhist wisdom, borne in the chant, which seeks always to go beyond all one-sidedness to nondualistic harmony.

This does not mean that Nichiren Shoshu would smooth over unsatisfactory aspects of national or family life, or be simply backward-looking. Rather, Nichiren Shoshu sees itself as the preparer of a new civilization, a civilization in which creative spontaneity will flourish. The real purpose of chanting is this; it is not to chant simply to get things on the material level. Nichiren Shoshu does not disdain material boons; it cannot, because one of its basic principles is that all levels of reality, what are called traditionally the Three Buddha "bodies" or forms of expression—absolute essence, the mental or "bliss" world, and the material—are really one. A cause implanted in one can produce an effect in another. There is no dualism; spiritual impulses can produce material goods; material goods can be related to mental happiness. In the same way, all time collapses into the present, the "real" time. And a person and his environment are one. For this reason, Nichiren Shoshu repudiates the notion that religion should be involved only in "spiritual" things or in happiness only in another world after death. But the main point of material benefits from chanting is that they show that this spiritual and material, past and future, self-environment interdependency is really true, that therefore Nichiren Shoshu really works and is incomparably profound.

Its goal is said to be world peace. This means that, after

enough people have been transformed by its practice, a new kind of world will have been created in which peace is possible. Wars and strife come out of human unhappiness. Abraham Maslow has told us we have two kinds of needs: deficiency needs and being needs. When we are frustrated, dissatisfied, lacking things that we feel we need, we have pathological relationships of aggression, weakness, or bitterness with others, either personally or nationally. The "being" state, however, is one of having no sense of need based on deficiency within the self; what goes out of one is only a "need" to love, relate, and create. It comes from strength and joy and confidence.

The Nichiren Shoshu chanting process, together with the supportive and very close fellowship of Nichiren Shoshu chapters, seeks to effect this kind of transformation. In many cases it has clearly succeeded. Its goal is nothing less than a world order grounded on this kind of person.

Such a world would obviously be very different from the present. The new civilization, significantly, is foretold not only in the chanting and the euphoria of chapter meetings but also in Nichiren Shoshu's cultural activities. The music, drama, and convention-planning activities are as much a part of what Nichiren Shoshu is trying to do as the chanting sessions. The two go together, like seed and flower.

In Japan, the organization sponsors a great number of professional middle-brow concerts for mass audiences at popular prices. This immensely successful program is called *min-on*. Moreover, the large Japanese young people's groups have gone to great length to develop amateur music and drama activities, enriching the lives of the workers and shopkeepers who make up the bulk of the Japanese membership.

In America, the same concerns are carried over. Professional *min-on* groups from Japan come to these shores and put on well-advertised concerts. Most American chapters also have amateur groups. Fife and drum corps, brass bands, and dance groups are favored, but chamber music, accordion, and singing groups are also found, as well as solo artists. The activities of all these groups are given great publicity and critical acclaim in the *World Tribune*; the glamour of greasepaint and footlights always hovers around the world of Nichiren Shoshu. The conventions, as has been noted, are great festivals of these talents, but increasingly performers stage independent concerts or take part in non-Nichiren Shoshu programs.

III

Where did this practice and outlook come from? Its roots, of course, are in the Buddhist tradition, and indeed Nichiren Shoshu claims to be "True Buddhism." Buddhism is a spiritual tradition hard to catch precisely in a word or phrase. Doubtless this is because one of its basic experiences is that anything which can be grasped, whether by hand or by the subtlest flitting thought, is partial, and the deep Buddha-wisdom, unattached and marvelous, empty of such crude tools as words, sees all things in equal relationship. Buddhism is sheer intuitive realization of the cosmic totality, which can be seen only when all blinders imposed by one's particular point of view fall away. Then one's true nature, and that of every other entity in this fluid and interlocking universe, comes into luminous view. This is the state of horizonless consciousness the Buddha attained at the hour of his enlightenment. In it, matter and mind, subject and object, merge into one unified field. One understands without words that he is a phenomenon, like all other conditioned things, flashing like a falling star through the unlimited and mysterious cosmic nature; he can let it sparkle with joy as it falls.

Among the greatest of Buddhist texts is the document called the Lotus Sutra. Attributed to the Buddha at the end of his ministry, it was probably actually composed several centuries later. It must present one of the most staggering vistas in all literature. The Buddha is pictured as enthroned on a mountaintop, surrounded by the Buddhas of millions and millions of other worlds and several categories of aspiring Buddhas.

The Lotus Sutra has the Buddha teach many things. One is that the whole mystery of the Buddha's work on earth, and the devices of the faith such as images and worship, are for the purpose of drawing one by charming enticements out of the danger of perishing from the fires of blind desire which obscure cosmic vision. A parable is told of a father who, seeing the house in which his children were playing catch fire, called them out of it not by shouting, which might have panicked or confused them, but by crying out that he had lovely new toys outdoors for them.

In the Lotus Sutra, the great teacher denigrates striving to attain enlightenment by strenuous effort, by thinking one can do it by arduous meditation or much study or good works done for the sake of selfish spiritual gain. He says that the simple offering of a child, making a temple of clay or bringing a crushed flower in his tiny hand to an image of the Buddha, comes out of a moment of sheer selfless devotion, and brings the infant devotee closer to enlightenment than those who struggle upward through seemingly more advanced means. The latter paradoxically build up their egos even as they try to lose them.

The wonderful mystery of the endless Buddha-cosmos,

replete with the lotus-enthroned Buddhas of a trillion worlds, is so far from the ken of our ordinary minds that the advance toward it that we make by the effort of study and forced meditation is only as an inch to a thousand miles; but if we just let go, like a child running to his mother with a handful of dandelions, or as in Nichiren Shoshu chanting, we are one with the Infinite simply because the mind has let fall all that cuts it off from infinity: ideas of separateness. Then we can flash onto an instant of unblinkered intuition. For the real secret is that we are part of this endless and splendid environment, and it is in us; we make it by seeing it, and it makes us. Therefore Nichiren Shoshu says *esho funi*, inner and outer are not two separate things; what is within our environment shapes us, until what is within our minds—as we internalize the joyful Buddha-reality—is instead potent enough to shape our environment.

Finally, the Lotus Sutra (in Chapter 10) tells of the Buddha's addressing a disciple, Bhaishagyaraga, commissioning him to preach the message, warning him of those who would persecute him but assuring him that the Buddha's protection will always remain with him. As though alluding to future time, the Buddha, in the verbose manner of this ancient scripture, speaks of the effect of veneration of the Lotus scripture itself:

> The Lord proceeded: Well, Bhaishagyaraga, all those Bodhisattvas Mahasattvas who in this assembly have heard, were it but a single stanza, a single verse or word, or who even by a single rising thought have joyfully accepted this Sutra, to all of them, Bhaishagyaraga, among the four classes of my audience I predict their destiny to supreme and perfect enlightenment. And to all whosoever, Bhaishagyaraga, who, after the complete extinction of the

Tathagata, shall hear this [teaching] and after hearing, were it but a single stanza, joyfully accept it, even with a single rising thought, to those also, Bhaishagyaraga, be they young men or young ladies of good family, I predict their destiny to supreme and perfect enlightenment. . . .

Those who shall take, read, make known, recite, copy, and after copying always keep in memory and from time to time regard were it but a single stanza of this [teaching]; who by that book shall feel veneration for the Tathagatas, treat then with the respect due to Masters, honour, revere, worship them; who shall worship that book with flowers, incense, perfumed garlands, ointment, powder, clothes, umbrellas, flags, banners, music, &c., and with acts of reverence such as bowing and joining hands; in short, Bhaishagyaraga, any young men or ladies of good family who shall keep or joyfully accept were it but a single stanza of this [teaching], to all of them, Bhaishagyaraga, I predict their being destined to supreme and perfect enlightenment.[15]

Then the Lotus Sutra (Chapter 11) tells of a glorious jeweled temple appearing, holding within it the greatest Buddha, the Buddha who is the cosmic essence itself. He is seen to be one with all Buddhas who have ever or will ever come to present these teachings on all worlds. The real Buddha was not one who was born, or who died, at any particular time; these are but garments he wore and will wear again, in a great game to draw children out of the fire.

The Lotus Sutra was among the most important scriptures in the Buddhist countries of China and Japan especially. It was held to be the supreme Buddhist statement by the T'ien T'ai (Tendai) monasteries. It was at the central monastery of this branch of Buddhism in Japan, at Mt. Hiei near Kyoto, that a young man who was to be called Nichiren studied at one stage of his career in the thirteenth century.

The vigorous activity of Nichiren Shoshu today scarcely fits the ordinary Western (and Eastern) image of Buddhism. Instead of rows of ethereal monks in silent meditation, here are smart, modern, businesslike people playing "pop" music, holding committee meetings, energetically cheering and chanting, scarcely pausing for "mindfulness" except that of the busy, happy present moment.

But if this is no ordinary Buddhism, neither was its central figure, the medieval Japanese monk and saint, Nichiren (1222–1282), a conventional Buddhist. He seems, rather, a combination of a transplanted Old Testament prophet, an intense Buddhist mystic, and Nietzsche's Zarathustra. He lived in the Kamakura period, when feudal warlords ruled Japan, though he seems really to have come into his own only in the twentieth century, amid economic explosions, "secular religion," "pop" mysticism, and much inner meaninglessness.

But thirteenth-century Japan was also a time of great change and disorder. The old imperial court in Kyoto, with its connections with the great Buddhist monasteries, had been supplanted for all practical purposes by a dynasty of warlords ruling from the city of Kamakura. People talked of the *mappo,* the last age of the Buddhist teaching, when no longer were there sages wise enough, or ascetics holy enough, to attain Buddhist liberation by study or practice of the scriptures. If one were to be saved at all in such a time, people said, it could be only by faith. The *mappo* idea was originally connected with an idea that times were getting worse and true faith was about to vanish from the earth until the coming of the next Buddha in the far-off future.

For Nichiren, though, the implications of *mappo* were quite otherwise. For him it meant the occasion for tremendous optimism. Liberation by faith only meant that now Buddhism was equally accessible to everyone, whether monk or peasant, wise or foolish. Therefore this was the time of the full release of true Buddhism into the world. And, rejecting the idea that the coming Buddha was remote, he believed that he was here now, in his own person. For this reason Nichiren is considered the Buddha of this age by Nichiren Shoshu.

The old Shingon and Tendai monasteries had tried to syncretize all human knowledge and experience into complex Buddhist systems. But the new Kamakura age had new spiritual needs, and new ideas seethed and bubbled in the warlord's world. There was a search for a Buddhism related to all of life, and to laymen as well as monks and courtiers. People wanted a simple key to the vast recondite mysteries of Buddhism. In the background was a prevailing pessimism.

Nichiren assumed that the Lotus Sutra held the answer somehow. But he was puzzled. He asked how it was that the imperial forces were defeated when they had with them the prayers and incantations of so many priests. He asked himself how one could be saved in such a time. His deep study and reflection on the Lotus Sutra led him to believe that it was the one truth needful, and that the old order had been defeated because it did not give the Lotus Sutra exclusive place. He also held that in the Lotus Sutra was contained a way to make all the power of Buddhism available to everyone. He saw it combining all areas of human experience into one simple unity, the goal of true Buddhism. All Buddhist promise and spiritual hope he saw collapsed into the radiant present, into the depths of the immediate, real world. Finally, he saw himself as the agent of this new message to the world, herald of a new and fabulously rich spiritual world. He identified himself with Visishtakarita (Jogyo), the leader of the host of bodhisattvas in the Lotus Sutra and the bearer of the eternal Buddha-light for this age.

He found himself saying, *"Nam Myoho Renge Kyo!"* These strange words have two levels of meaning. They can mean, "Hail to the marvelous wisdom of the Lotus Sutra." Nichiren Shoshu, however, puts far more emphasis on the subtler meaning, "Dedication to the Wondrous Essence and the Phenomenal World United!" Or, as they put it, "Devotion to the Mystic Law of Cause and Effect Through Sound!" To understand why it means this takes some knowledge of Buddhist philosophy and the symbolic language associated with it, in which Buddha-wisdom is the essence of the universe, the changeless absolute, and the many-petaled lotus is the phenomenal world of appearance, change, and multiplicity, of simultaneous cause and effect.

The point is that in the chant these two are united, the inner and the outer, mind and body, and in this union is all power and all bliss. And this chant, Nichiren realized, was something anyone could do at any time. It meant a transformation of Buddhism, as though he and the chant were a funnel to release into the world a single, clear light. There is, he said, one sutra, one practice, one time, one man (himself), and one country (Japan) as points of reference for the new Buddhism. This radical simplification is the key to his "secularization" of Buddhism, for by bringing the transcendent referrent down to one point, all the things in the world are equally related to it, as the rim of a wheel to its axle. One can relate to the essence as well in the fields or a shop as in a monastic temple.

On fire with this message, Nichiren went into Japan a fervent advocate and teacher. With the vigor of modern Nichiren Shoshu people, he called on Japan to repent. He attacked other religions and other forms of Buddhism because he believed that disasters had come upon Japan as a result of their not adhering strictly and exclusively to the Lotus teaching. He was exiled, nearly executed (his followers believed his last-minute reprieve was miraculous), and vindicated when a Mongol invasion he had foretold came to pass. He was the kind of strong, unavoidable person who makes fervent disciples and angry enemies.

Besides chanting the "*Nam Myoho Renge Kyo*," called the Daimoku, Nichiren taught that two other things were essential to his faith. One is the Gohonzon, the already-mentioned paper used as an object of worship. The characters inscribed on it are the names of the principle Buddhas and bodhisattvas in the Lotus Sutra. Like the chant, it encapsulates the infinite riches of the Lotus Sutra, and of the infinite reality behind it, into small compass. It goes with the Daimoku by providing a visual complement to its audial expression, and an object of focus. It is not said to be an object of worship as though it were a god outside oneself, a very non-Buddhist idea, but a way of "turning on" the true object of worship, which is within. A recent issue of the *World Tribune* says:

> That the Gohonzon is a correct object of worship in no way makes it restrictive. Because it is purely representative of the human life, its sole function is to allow that life to blossom in a myriad of ways simultaneously. The estab-

lishment of a Third Civilization created by men, all of whom are fully realizing and utilizing the beauty of their own lives, is the goal of Nichiren Shoshu.[16]

Thus the Gohonzon really represents the individual worshiper. It is like a mirror, imaging in mantic Buddha-names the vast riches of the infinite Buddha-nature within him as it is released by the chant. As one member put it, the Gohonzon, like coffee at 6 A.M., has life—but it has only the life that we put into it. Don't look, he said, for the power of the Gohonzon outside yourself.

The third great principle of Nichiren is the Kaidan (literally, "ordination platform"). Because he thought the existent forms of Buddhism were not able to carry true Buddhism in the new age, Nichiren felt it necessary to establish his own denomination, headquarters, and spiritual succession.

The idea of a specific place as the terrestrial focal point of the movement is represented in Nichiren Shoshu by the impressive headquarters at the foot of Mt. Fuji, where the new Sho-Hondo was opened in 1972. The role that pilgrimage to the headquarters plays in Nichiren Shoshu, together with the role of centralized organization and an international perspective symbolized by pilgrimage, is of equal importance to most members with chanting and Gohonzon. One can tell this from the amount of talk and column space in the *World Tribune* given to the headquarters, the movement's leadership, and journeys to Japan. All of this is part of the expression of the Kaidan principle.

The work of Nichiren left several denominations in its wake. Of these, the one called Nichiren Shoshu (literally, "Nichiren True Teaching"), affirmed that it was the legitimate custodian of his work on the basis of its possessing not only the correct teaching but also the Gohonzon said to have been made by Nichiren and other relics, such as Nichiren's tooth.

IV

The life of Nichiren Shoshu was relatively quiet for several centuries. The beginning of its remarkable modern upsurge was in 1928 when a Japanese schoolteacher and educational philosopher named Tsunesaburo Makiguchi was converted to it, along with a younger disciple, Josei Toda (1900–1958). Two years later, in 1930, they founded a group called Sokagakkai (literally, "Value-Creation Society"; its first name was Soka Kyoiku Gakkai, "Value-Creation Education Society"). Its outlook was based on Nichiren Shoshu teachings and Makiguchi's own educational philosophy. Makiguchi held, in brief, that the traditional triad of values of Western philosophy, attributed to Kant, of Goodness, Beauty, and Truth, should be amended to Goodness, Beauty, and Benefit, for not all that is true is of use to man's needs, but benefit *is* by definition. This was a way of saying that the goal of education should be the good of the individual and society, not just an abstract ideal of truth.

If the "true" means just what is factual, it is an impossible goal anyway, since any content we give the term is based only on limited human observation and experience. But we can know what of reality is of benefit to man. One can see how this pragmatic philosophy fits in with Nichiren's teaching that the true Buddhism of the Lotus Sutra means a uniting of all realms of Buddha-nature in the present as a source of power for a joyful, prosperous life here and now.

Sokagakkai was not formally a religious movement. In

the 1930's it was just a small discussion group and, for a time, a magazine. However, it was composed mostly of Nichiren Shoshu members. But in 1942 the wartime Japanese government, avid for totalitarian control over all areas of thought and association, tried to force it to unite with the other Nichiren sects. In 1943, Makiguchi and Toda were imprisoned for refusal to participate in Shinto worship. Makiguchi died in prison the following year.

Toda was released on parole in July 1945. His followers now believe that he attained supreme enlightenment while in prison. Immediately upon his release, in the waning days of the war, he began to contact remaining members and reconstruct the organization of Sokagakkai. The coming of religious freedom under the Occupation gave him wider opportunity. In 1951, Toda became officially president of Nichiren Shoshu Sokagakkai, a group now constituted as a lay teaching and evangelistic organization within the Nichiren Shoshu denomination. At the same time the group significantly began work on a new Daisekiji, or headquarters temple for the faith, at Mt. Fuji.

Under Toda's postwar leadership, the distinctive ideas of Makiguchi's philosophy became less and less Sokagakkai's *raison d'être,* though they were used more or less homiletically in expressing reasons why people should enter Nichiren Shoshu practice. Rather, Sokagakkai, with the freedom of a lay movement, was an evangelistic agency for Nichiren Shoshu. But it had its own structure, its own meetings for worship and cultural life, its own chain of command, its own publications. So successful was it that soon it had five times the membership of the rest of Nichiren Shoshu, a strange relationship between a denomination and its working arm, but one that has been mutually fruitful.

Under Toda's fervent and utterly dedicated leadership, Sokagakkai attained tremendous prominence. In the 1950's it was often called the fastest-growing religion in the world. In his inaugural address in 1951, when he had only a tiny band of followers, Toda vowed to attain a membership of 750,000 households in seven years. In 1957 it was announced that this goal had been reached. The following year Toda died, the day after he returned from the dedication of a new lecture hall at the head temple. Now the movement claims 7,500,000 families.

Apart from the power of the practice and teaching, the growth was accomplished by thorough organization, aggressive selling by members, and the image that Sokagakkai projected of a wholly modern, streamlined version of Buddhism put before a traditionally Buddhist nation, but one in which older forms of Buddhism, as of Shinto, had been discredited by the disaster of the war.

Sokagakkai was organized into prefectural, city, district, and block groups. Each member was expected personally to practice *shakubuku* (literally, "break and subdue," i.e., "to break one's hold on old Buddhist beliefs and instill the cause of happiness"), as the recruitment of new members was called. In the 1950's, in its eagerness to establish a large base, Sokagakkai, it was said, used intolerant, unfair arguments against other religions, and used various forms of pressure to win and hold converts. Yet the zealotry worked, and as membership grew rapidly, so did a diversity of cultural and social expressions. Sokagakkai developed large youth organizations, and it is the only religion to make much impact on postwar Japan's restless, rootless, searching young people. Sokagakkai was able to get hundreds of thousands of them into vast rallies, with chants, cheers, marching groups, and banners. In its crusade for the soul of the nation, Sokagakkai also established the *min-on* popular music groups. In all of this it was, of course, intruding on territory already staked out by Marxist student and labor groups. Sokagakkai fought and sometimes won titanic battles with Marxist-oriented unions and youth groups. It made much use of newspapers and mass media.

Of course, Sokagakkai incurred much criticism, and still does, in Japan. It is accused of fanaticism, high-pressure tactics, mixing religion and politics through its political party, the Komeito, and of inculcating a protofascist, "true believer" mentality. Yet familiarity with the wartime sufferings, and the crisis of values in postwar Japan, can help one to see its role in better perspective. I once visited the home of a woman in Tokyo whose child I had been supporting through the Christian Children's Fund. Upon entering the home, I found that (although the child had been attending a Christian school) the living room was dominated by a huge Gohonzon, and the mother pressed some Sokagakkai literature into my hands. She had lost all her own family to the atomic bomb at Hiroshima and had since been abandoned by her husband. She now supported herself and her child by selling newspapers on the street corner. But she had a perpetual optimism and cheerfulness. I am sure she is much borne up by her Nichiren Shoshu faith, and by the care of other members in her neighborhood.

The real sociological strength of Sokagakkai lies in the tightness of its neighborhood groups, in which there is continual contact, jobs to be done, and mutual help. This is much in contrast to the rather remote image that traditional Shinto and Buddhism offer most common people. Sokagakkai may be overpersistent, yet it probably took real zeal for conversions and thorough organization down to the block level to reach a person like this woman, and to give meaning and joy to what otherwise must have been an empty and hopeless life.

Toda was succeeded in 1960 by Daisaku Ikeda, apparently through a process of emergent leadership rather than by general election. His era of leadership has been marked by certain shifts, and Toda is reported now to have said just before his end, "After my death, you can erase what I have said and start out with a clean slate." The intense promotional methods that had engendered criticism have been modified to encourage a gentler spirit and give a more humanistic image. The cultural promise of Nichiren Shoshu, as the release of a new civilization, has been emphasized. In his November 2, 1971, presidential address to the 34th General Meeting, for example, Ikeda said that culture is the "incarnation of religion." This address was the Magna Carta of the present movement toward understanding Nichiren Shoshu life as "true humanism." Surveying magisterially the scope of human culture East and West, Ikeda concluded that what is required of "a culture which begins and ends with man" is harmony, which in turn depends on a complete view of human existence. This "complete view" will see man, culture, and the cosmos as harmonious parts of a vast totality. Only Nichiren's Buddhism, with its great principle of *ichinen sanzen* ("One Mind in the three thousand things," or "Three thousand conditions of life in a momentary state of existence"), can provide the total perspective necessary. But to spread it, Nichiren Buddhism must be shown in its cultural manifestation, that is, as cultural progress. In this process, each nation must maintain and develop its own culture while merging into a cosmic harmony of unity in diversity. To demonstrate this is true *kosen rufu,* propagation of True Buddhism, and a true "total revolution." [17]

President Ikeda's 1972 presidential address, given on November 2 of that year, carried the same ideas farther. Alluding to the tremendous and increasing domination of modern man's life by technological and political forces, he called for greater attention to the philosophical basis for belief in the value of human life, and an enhancement of demonstration of its value by cultural enrichment. He then entered into a breathtaking projection of the future. He saw the years 2001–2050 as a period when, with the help of Nichiren Shoshu's growth, a "peace formidable enough to prevent the annihilation of the human race" must be built. Particularly, he hoped, these would be years of happiness for Asia, which has suffered so much in the twentieth century. Then, the years from 2051–2100, marking the hundredth anniversary of the Sho-Hondo, can be the years in which Nichiren's philosophy is recognized as "the contemporary expression of the times." Then, in the period 2101–2150, he said he would "like to see the indestructible foundation of a permanent peace completed." And in 2151–2200, "every aspect of Kosen-rufu will hopefully be brought to perfection." [18]

All this spells out at least that Nichiren Shoshu sees itself in the present world as being the seed of a different and far better future. In this day of so much pessimism about man's political, economic, and ecological future, it is striking to see a prediction couched in such different and more optimistic terms. Certainly Nichiren Shoshu is an anomaly among spiritual movements in the world. While many others, especially other forms of Buddhism, are stagnant and backward-looking, it is growing, casts about it a very modern image, and talks of a splendid future. By seeking to work out of an area of human life between the conflicting political and technological forces of today, it wants to nourish an alternative spirituality and life-style to take over when their day is past. It may be so; the basic motifs of new cycles of civilization often seem obscure, even irrelevant, during their early years when they still lie buried in the bosom of the dying previous cycle.

This is one light in which we can view the Sokagakkai-related political party in Japan, the Komeito, formed early in the years of Ikeda's presidency. It is intended to implement Sokagakkai ideals in national life, and has become Japan's third largest party, though this development too, understandably, has aroused controversy. Thus far, the Komeito has done much exposing of corruption in the government in power and has taken a moderately leftist position on issues such as welfare and the presence of American bases in Japan, while strongly affirming (as the Socialist opposition does not) traditional Japanese cultural values. The Komeito is technically independent of both Sokagakkai and Nichiren Shoshu. There is no reason to think that American Nichiren Shoshu members particularly identify with its political positions or feel that a similar political wing would be appropriate in this country.

With all these factors combined, Sokagakkai in Japan today presents an image of being the most highly organized religious-cultural group in the nation, one offering an alternative to Marxism and sheer materialism, yet advocating something of the former's fervor for a new kind of man in a new social order, and something of the latter's belief that poverty is not the answer and that life is meant to be enjoyed. It appears as the dispenser of all sorts of social and cultural goods for everyone. It offers meetings

and activities in which even the lowliest can have acceptance and a sense of importance—concerts and sports
events and rallies for all, and a feeling that someone cares.
It appears involved in all areas of national life—politics,
mass media, culture. Behind all of this, of course, it appears as a body with a singular belief in a simple spiritual
practice with a rather arcane Buddhist philosophy behind
it, one that relates its modernity to the wonderful aura of
mystic profundity which dwells in the treasured ancient
Buddhist temples of Japan. Both are presented as the best
and most direct way to the full release of all latent potential for joy, power, and liberation.

In sum, Sokagakkai, and Nichiren Shoshu as revitalized
by it, appears as a modern movement deeply rooted in
Japan's medieval and Buddhist past, with its mysterious
Gohonzon, incense, and great temple at the foot of Mt.
Fuji, the very symbol of Japan, where traditional Buddhist
priests still chant in the ancient manner on behalf of this
streamlined faith. The dedication of the new Sho-Hondo
in 1972 was emblematic of bringing all these strands together.

V

It was under Ikeda's leadership that this puissant faith
of many strands was officially rooted in America. The first
Occidental Americans brought into it were GI's influenced
by Japanese girl friends and wives. Back in the United
States, returning servicemen, their wives, and some Japanese-Americans who practiced Nichiren Buddhism infor-
mally met together during the 1950's. It was not until 1960,
however, that Ikeda came to America to set the movement on a regular footing in the New World. He said upon
landing: "We have now made the first footprint on this

continent as did Christopher Columbus. Yet we face even a greater task than he in driving home the wedge on this tour. Twenty or fifty years from now, this day will be marked as one of great importance."

From then on, fortuitously aided by the yeasty spiritual atmosphere of the 1960's, the work flourished. In 1961 the first pilgrimage to Japan by Americans was made to the Daisekiji, the head temple at the foot of Mt. Fuji. Sixty-eight participated; in 1972 eighteen hundred went to Japan from America for the dedication of the new Sho-Hondo. In 1963 the Los Angeles Kaikan ("Headquarters") of Sokagakkai was established, the first in the world outside of Japan. The man behind the growth was Masayasu Sadanaga, who, in order to strengthen the American identity of Nichiren Shoshu in this country, had his name legally changed to George M. Williams in 1972.

Mr. Sadanaga/Williams was born of a Japanese family in Seoul, Korea, in 1930. His family, impoverished by the war, returned to Japan in 1945. He got a job as an elevator operator in a United States Air Force building. The job of being servant to the victors involved its humiliations, but a few officers befriended the young Japanese and helped him enter Meiji University, where he received a degree in law. He got into Sokagakkai in 1953 when his mother joined, and he rapidly became active in the burgeoning movement. In 1957 he came to America, where he did graduate work at UCLA, George Washington University, and the University of Maryland. He organized the first American Sokagakkai group in Washington, D.C., and devoted himself to contacting Sokagakkai people in America, many of whom were lonely and unhappy Japanese "war brides." When President Ikeda came to America in 1960, it was Sadanaga who greeted him; he had worked with Ikeda in Japan in the Sokagakkai youth division before Ikeda's accession in 1960. It was natural that Sadanaga should have been given the leadership of the American work. He has been an active, busy, caring leader, covering one hundred thousand miles a year in travel. For example, on hearing of President Kennedy's assassination in 1963, he immediately flew to Texas to be with Nichiren Shoshu members there and chant to complete Kennedy's work.

That same year, 1963, the first national convention was held in Chicago. Fifteen hundred members attended. The next year, 1964, there were thirteen chapters, and the newspaper, the *World Tribune*, was begun. (It now has a circulation of forty thousand.) The October 17, 1964, issue tells the story of a New York woman who said her ulcer was healed through chanting—an emphasis on healing still stressed today. The *World Tribune* for September 15, 1972, contains an account of a girl suffering from the aftereffects of Mediterranean fever, which gave her intense pain at times and required a milk-free diet. She was cured, the story says, while chanting in the presence of President Ikeda. All this is part of the Nichiren Shoshu concept that a renewal of the whole person brings physical benefits in its train.

The attempt to relate to American history was also already a motif in 1964; another early article, "Frontier Spirit Paves Way for Kosen Rufu [propagation of True Buddhism] of America," relates that America was settled by people seeking happiness and a better way of life, and that the teachings of Nichiren are the culmination of that quest. "America has been waiting for the Sokagakkai. One by one, families are being awakened to the truth, the way to true happiness. The Sokagakkai is sowing the seeds of the True Civilization as Nichiren Daishonin has taught us. Sunshine has come to America. Just as, 'Spring is sure to follow, after a hard, cold, long winter.' " One feels that something of the promise of this was fulfilled when he reads a story like that in the September 18, 1972 issue, of the leaders of a multiracial, multinational settlement house in New York, a house packed with the progeny of seekers of the American dream, who took to chanting and taking part in *min-on* activities. One teacher, Maria Gonzales, says it is only chanting that gives her the strength to do her job.

In 1965 another national convention was held, this time in Los Angeles, with twenty-three hundred present. The *World Tribune* began reporting one thousand *shakubuku* results—i.e., conversions—a month. By 1966 the *World Tribune* was reporting that America was number one in the world in *shakubuku* statistics, or in rate of membership growth per member.

The cultural side of the movement was being enhanced too. On June 16, 1966, the headlines of the *World Tribune* screamed, "AMERICA THRILLED BY MIN-ON," and featured articles on the first visit by a group of *min-on* performers from Japan, who put on a show called "Holiday in Tokyo." Singers, one called "Perry Como in miniature," dancers, and combo music were offered.

The headline may have been a bit hyperbolic, but the importance of this event for Nichiren Shoshu of America would be hard to overestimate. Both here and in Japan, *min-on* is the "culture for the masses" side of Nichiren Shoshu. In America, its meaning is freedom and creativity as tokens of the new Nichiren Shoshu man. Ikeda said, "If anything can revitalize the barren hearts of people and unite the hearts of all the world, it must be music." *Min-on* typifies Nichiren Shoshu's view that religion is not just religion, it is a whole cultural and (in Japan) political program at once creating and expressing a new humanism. In America it takes such forms as noontime concerts in shopping malls, marching in convention parades, and months of practicing together. Nowadays the *World Tribune* is full of accounts of Nichiren Shoshu units taking part in parades and local celebrations of all sorts everywhere: rodeos, small-town centennials, and rock festivals.

In 1967 the character of the American movement changed somewhat. The first Nichiren Shoshu priest arrived from Japan to establish a temple, thus legitimizing the American work of Sokagakkai as a branch of the traditional Nichiren Shoshu denomination. The work became officially Nichiren Shoshu of America, and the term Sokagakkai was no longer used here. There are now three temples in America: in Washington, D.C.; in Etiwanda in southern California; and in Hawaii. These temples and their priests handle ceremonies such as formal weddings and consecrations of Gohonzons. Also in 1967, the famous Nichiren Shoshu fife and drum corps and brass band gave their first concerts, and a convention was held in San Francisco. An even more significant landmark: in the concern to make Nichiren Shoshu truly American, since 1967 meetings in the Japanese language (except of course for chanting and Gongyo) have been forbidden. Occidentals now occupy positions on all levels of leadership. In respect to language and leadership, Nichiren Shoshu is the most Americanized of the Japanese New Religions.

In 1968 a convention was held in Hawaii, a congenial environment. The first of a series of academic seminars on campuses for university students was conducted by Mr. Sadanaga.

Those were days of fantastic growth for Nichiren Shoshu. By 1969 the movement had 114 chapters and the *shakubuku* rate had reached 7,854 a month. An article in *Life* magazine (January 9, 1970) stated that two hundred thousand Americans were in Nichiren Shoshu.

Who were these people? An analysis published by the World Tribune Press[19] indicates that, as of 1970, about a quarter were in southern California; the rest were scattered across the nation, with heavy concentrations in New York, Washington, D.C., Chicago, Seattle, San Francisco, and Hawaii.

By age, the membership broke down in this way:

20 or younger—17%
21–30— 40%
31–40— 19%
41–50— 15%
51–60— 6%
61 or older— 3%

It is evident that Nichiren Shoshu is predominantly a youth movement, but by no means exclusively so.

In the same year, Nichiren Shoshu was 59% female, 41% male; 47% were married, 40% single, 9% divorced, and 4% widows or widowers.

Ethnic origin represented a marked shift from Oriental preponderance. In 1970, Nichiren Shoshu of America was 41% Caucasian, 30% Oriental, 12% black, 13% Latin-American, and 4% other. This may be compared with 1960, when the movement was 96% Oriental, and 1965, when the Oriental membership was 77% of the total.

Family religion before joining Nichiren Shoshu represented a similar spread. In 1970, it was Catholic 30%, Protestant 30%, Buddhist 25%, Jewish 6%, other 4%, atheist

5%. The Protestant category broke down to Baptist 40%, Methodist 19%, Presbyterian 9%, Episcopalian 8%, Lutheran 7%, other 17%.

As to employment of Nichiren Shoshu members, in 1970 it included:

Housewife 27%	Technical 8%
Student 19%	Executive 4%
Unskilled 6%	Professional 10%
Blue collar 9%	Other 7%
Clerical 10%	

It is indeed not mainly the mighty of the earth Nichiren Shoshu has most deeply touched and made builders of the new civilization. One reads continually in the *World Tribune* of people whose lives have been transformed—a retired sailor, a young man once involved with a pack of racketeers, runaway young people, the sick and outcast, a barber whose life had been blank and almost suicidal. But these are now weaving in their lives the fabric of a new humanity, a new culture.

Yet as the decade of the 1970's opened, and the spiritual climate in America shifted subtly from the expansive experimentalism of the 1960's to an inward-looking mood typified by the Jesus movement, Nichiren Shoshu of America entered into a period of retrenchment and change. Even though it had done much to help people move from the extreme alienation characteristic of the 1960's to reacceptance of American values, it could not compete with evangelical Christianity as a voice of the American past and symbolic bearer of the American spiritual heritage. Many fair-weather friends of Nichiren fell away, and aggressive styles of *shakubuku* turned counterproductive in some places.

By late 1972, though, Nichiren Shoshu was on the move again, and new members were coming in. The image was changed in some ways. "Solicitation" often replaced *shakubuku*. There was less emphasis on immediate healing and material benefits from chanting, more on serious points of Buddhist philosophy and above all on the experience as a release of creative personality potential. The 1973 convention was held in Japan.

The attitude toward Nichiren Shoshu's Judeo-Christian environment had also gone great lengths toward openness. In the early 1950's, Sokagakkai in Japan published a *shakubuku* manual presenting extremely harsh arguments against Christianity and other religions, and saying that to join Nichiren Shoshu one must destroy all shrines and traces of other faiths in home and heart, even as Makiguchi refused to worship at a Shinto shrine. But it is now said that Nichiren Shoshu is a "philosophy" and one can practice it and still be a good Protestant, Catholic, or Jew. It is said that in a non-Buddhist country such as America, Nichiren Shoshu comes only to embellish other faiths, not to replace them. Thus the very word *shakubuku*, associated in many minds with the old "hard-line" approach, is less used, at least in America.

VI

What is the doctrine of Nichiren Shoshu? Spokesmen for Nichiren Shoshu of America emphasize that it has no mandatory doctrine, despite all the philosophical insights that are presented in lectures. It has never published a catechism or dogmatic statement. The only purpose, one is told, is to chant and accomplish one's own goals, and develop humanity to levels beyond the ken of any creed. It is true that most Nichiren Shoshu people are not very much attuned to theory. They don't want to convince people on historical or philosophical grounds, but just on the basis of "Try it. If 'Nam Myoho Renge Kyo' works for you, keep on doing it and spread it."

Nevertheless, the introductory lectures make statements that are fundamental to traditional Nichiren Shoshu apologetics, and express in Buddhist language the basic experience, which is that life is one and must be lived beautifully in the present moment.

The goal is harmony: the point of chanting is to put oneself in harmony with the universe, to open up that deep part of the self which is always akin to all that is and which nothing can impede. One leading member told me that while other faiths set up a dichotomy between religion and life, and so talk about bringing Jesus *into* business and so forth, in Nichiren Shoshu there is no way to separate them. If it doesn't influence all life and thought, it isn't working at all; chanting should be like eating and breathing.

The Nichiren Shoshu tradition says there are ten basic states of life: hellish suffering, the incessant hunger of wandering ghosts, animality, angry titans, human tranquillity, heavenly rapture (the six traditional Buddhist planes where karmic reincarnation is possible), learning, following the path, aspiration for enlightenment, the supreme bliss of Buddhahood (four traditional stages of the spiritual ascent). These are all conditions of the *present*, Nichiren said, not afterlife conditions or parts of a long saga. A person may move through all ten several times in one day. But they can all be brought into "one thought" by the chanting of the Daimoku.

This radical drive toward unification of all realities earthly and spiritual into one experience in the immediate present is the energizing power of Nichiren Shoshu. Its possibility and awesome bliss are the secret of Nichiren Shoshu. This unity is caught up in several key phrases: *esho funi*, "subject and object are not two"; *inga guji*, "simultaneous cause and effect" or karma; *shikishin funi*, "body and mind are not two"; *obutsu myogo*, "King and Buddha (or society and religion) a single unity." A civilization in which these seeming polarities were all resolved would surely be one in which man could be realized.

Nichiren likewise taught that the three traditional expressions of the Buddha-nature—as essence of the universe, as heavenly lord, and as earthly teacher of saving wisdom—must be brought together. Other forms of Buddhism, he said, emphasized one at the expense of the other two. But his was a Buddhism not of heaven and meditation but of a radical simplicity and unity here and now in the release of the chant, when all potentialities are realized in one moment which is the present.

The Nichiren tradition has also said there are three proofs for any religion or philosophy: the documentary, the theoretical, and the practical. Does it use an authentic scriptural source? Is it logical and intellectually viable? Does it stand the test of daily life? Nichiren Shoshu people are convinced that their teaching passes each of these tests handsomely, but like Nichiren himself they insist the last should be the most decisive. Many religions can appear plausible in arguments from scripture or philosophy, but do they really deliver the goods in the ordinary problems of life?

The real emphasis in Nichiren Shoshu is on happiness. Nothing really matters except the radiant, vital faces so characteristic of its people. This is the real meaning of *ichinen sanzen:* one thought, in the present moment. A

Newsweek article about Nichiren Shoshu was rightly entitled "Happy Talk." [20] George Williams says, "Happy individuals can build a happy nation and a happy world."

The organization is difficult to characterize, since it gives an impression of being both tight and loose at once. Perhaps the most accurate statement would be to say it is a close-knit community. Formally, organization works from the top down. The general director of Nichiren Shoshu of America, George Williams, is also editor of the thrice-weekly paper, *World Tribune.* He is responsible to President Ikeda in Japan and the Sokagakkai there; the three American temples are independent of this structure. Under Mr. Williams is a board of directors which handles departments of publications, the *World Tribune, min-on,* finance, conventions, pilgrimages, the academy, and public relations.

The basic unit of the geographical divisions is the district, which meets several times a week and is under the leadership of a district chief, who is typically a persistent "go-getter" type of person. The larger regional unit is the chapter; the district may be divided into smaller "groups" and "units." It is on this level that the community spirit is a part of one's daily experience. Members may expect to be kept in close touch with district and chapter events by phone calls and visits. Districts will have frequent goals or competitions for selling the *World Tribune* and getting people to conventions and special events. Members will be expected to practice chanting and Gongyo daily and to be at meetings frequently. Nichiren Shoshu is a time-consuming thing, but a thing in which one is never alone.

The happiness of Nichiren Shoshu, then, is not hereafter but here and now. The *Newweek* article may have been incorrect in saying Nichiren Shoshu is "neither exotic nor mysterious"—at least my impression of Gongyo could be described by these adjectives—but certainly it is not intended as a foretaste of heaven, a magical salvation rite, or an inducer of classical mystical states of consciousness. Rather, it is as practical as plumbing, an act that is experienced as releasing power, spiritual energy, exuberant vitality, for radiant and effective living in the here and now. A person who has this power may well double his salary, as some have reported, but basically that is because he is inwardly renewed—because he is a new person worth twice as much.

It is evidently a secular faith. It is rightly called "humanistic" when really understood. All the promises of religion are made to apply to this world. All divine potential is within man, it is said, and can be unleashed. The view of the scope of human capability is one that modern psychology is just beginning to scan in its study of states of consciousness, transpersonal psychology, and so forth. According to the Buddhism of Nichiren Shoshu, chanting is really the way the marvelous Buddha-nature, the ground of the safe haven which is our universe, can manifest itself in all the phenomenal world.

READING SELECTION

The following selection, from an NSA Handbook, describes the Nichiren Shoshu conventions. In a peculiar way, this passage seems to sum up the stirring sense of happiness and vitality that is so much at the core of the Nichiren Shoshu experience in America.

A Nichiren Shoshu convention is so much more than what the word "convention" suggests. From an overall viewpoint it seems to be a celebration, and, in a very real sense, it is a celebration of the joy of living a victorious life. As thousands upon thousands of members gather, sharing individual experiences of benefit from their practice of True Buddhism, there's a natural buildup of enthusiastic energy far above the normal level for a life-sized crowd. This overwhelming happiness is so contagious that it literally sweeps visitors and guests off their feet and leaves them with a lasting impression of Nichiren Shoshu's positive power.

This is a power which envelops and surrounds anyone and everyone within the sphere of convention activities. During the Seattle Convention in 1971, the *Seattle Post-Intelligencer* reported that "A Seattle motorcycle policeman who zipped down the street before the parade was surprised to find himself the sole recipient of a resounding 7,000 voice acclaim. And when a Seattle Engineering Department truck came through to remove the street clearing signs for the middle of Fourth Avenue, a voice from the loudspeaker broke out with: 'Let's have a big hand for the orange truck clearing all the obstacles.'"

The happiness generated by a convention affects the entire city in which it takes place. In Seattle, Ray Ruppert, Religion Editor of the *Post-Intelligencer,* noted that ". . . They'll be spreading that happiness and joy around Seattle today and tomorrow with a parade, fireworks, art exhibits and so on to which Nichiren Shoshu has invited the general public. A skeptic might think that there's almost too much happiness around the Nichiren Shoshu Convention. . . . But then, the skeptic can be reminded that in the religious thinking of our day, celebration is a form of religious expression too."

Naturally, these gigantic assemblies are a great encour-

agement to the members as well. What each person is able
to derive from some aspect of the convention is perhaps
the most important factor and explains why the total effect
is so significant. One young mother remembered the 1969
Washington, D.C., Convention as the turning point in her
family's happiness. Years of disagreement and hurt feelings between her and her father seemed to melt away as
they stood together at the "Parade of Happiness."

"We had the most marvellous time together," she re-
members, "as the parade passed by—not just watching,
but encouraging them and feeling involved, really a part
of it. We were laughing together like we hadn't done in
years, and the closeness we had felt for each other before
came back."

As vivid proof of its fantastic expansion and power to
make so many people happy, events of such scale promote
the first chance to actually see the enormous size of the
organization. Up until the convention, perhaps they would
only hear of NSA, but once they actually see thousands of
members assembled from all over the country, the whole
concept becomes much more realistic and easy to believe.

It takes many different colored flowers to comprise a
beautiful garden. Even a tiny flower has a mission to bud
and sink its roots into the soil. There is a harmonious pattern discernible throughout nature as we carefully observe
the phenomena around us. Even within the body, quite a
few different organs coordinate to support the processes
of life and growth.

In the same way, true unity means individual people
working together, living together and building together
for the peace and happiness of the entire world. A Nichiren Shoshu convention symbolizes many things. People
come from every corner of the continent, from Canada,

Panama, Mexico and the United States. Every one of them contributes to the success of the event.

Some people come to sing, others to dance. Some work behind the stage, others march in a parade or enter a painting in an art exhibition. The success of the convention relies on each person's effort. Thus far, the efforts of thousands of people over the last several years have created huge successes in Chicago, New York, Los Angeles and Hawaii, climaxing with the fantastic Seattle Convention in July, 1971, with 10,000 participants. Future conventions are scheduled for Mexico City, Philadelphia, Boston and several other cities throughout the continent. These will bring the blossoming organization of NSA closer to all the people of America.

These coming years will mark the new beginnings of real happiness for the American people. Strongly united and unwavering in its determination to let all mankind know about this life-philosophy, NSA will continue to take giant leaps forward, under the direction of President Daisaku Ikeda. It is dedicating unsparing efforts to infuse humanism back into the society and to allow people everywhere to enjoy the fruits of the happiest possible life.

—NSA Handbook No. 1, *What Is Nichiren Shoshu?* Compiled by the World Tribune Press from the notes and lectures of George M. Williams, General Director of Nichiren Shoshu of America (Santa Monica: World Tribune Press, 1971), pp. 36–41.

4
The Church
of World Messianity

I

The incoming of the Direct Light of God to inaugurate a
New Age . . . Johrei . . . nature farming . . . consciousness of beauty . . . the building of miniature paradises—
these are major themes of the Church of World Messianity. This faith was started in Japan under a different name
in 1935 by Mokichi Okada as a result of revelations given
to him earlier. He died in 1955. Since 1950, he has been
called by his followers Meishu-sama, "Enlightened Lord."
The religion has shown fluctuations in reputation and
membership, but is now on an upswing. Despite cultish
beginnings, it has produced a not unsophisticated world
view comparable to Neoplatonism, and seems to have
found the secret of making contact with some of the most
deeply felt spiritual needs of many American youth.

In 1974, World Messianity claimed 700,000 adherents
worldwide, up from 400,000 a decade earlier. Even more
significant, during that decade it made its first noticeable
impact in the West.

Of its 700,000 members, 650,000 are in Japan, where
there are 43 central churches, one in each prefecture or
major geographical area. In Brazil the faith claims some

40,000 members, 70 percent of Occidental descent. The U.S. membership in 1974 was 3,500, half of whom are in Hawaii and are mostly Japanese. Of the 1,750 or so on the mainland, about one third are of Japanese ancestry and two thirds are Caucasian. But of the 1,100 or so Occidental adherents (a figure up by 300 from 1972), half are under thirty years of age, whereas the average age of Japanese members is around fifty. There are four or five blacks in World Messianity.

These figures do not fully indicate the role that the Church of World Messianity is playing in America. Many people have heard the name of its central spiritual practice, Johrei (spiritual purification), and the effect it is said to have on the healing of mind and body. Johrei is discussed among young people aware of "underground" spiritual movements and older spiritual seekers alike. Many who have not felt able to join the Church of World Messianity formally have received Johrei, and some receive it regularly.

Still others have been impressed by the fact that World Messianity's ideas about the spiritual changes going on in the world now correspond to popular talk about the Aquarian Age or the New Age—and that in Johrei there is a practice which is said to channel straight to individuals the New Age forces of Direct Light now coming into the world in preparation for the creation of paradise on earth. Yet others, influenced by the vogue for health foods and ecology, are interested in World Messianity's important teachings about "nature farming."

Nonetheless, the individual healing and purifying rite of Johrei is the central attraction of the Church of World Messianity, at least at first for most outside inquirers.

At my first experience of Johrei, I was seated in the nave of the church, facing a simple, expressive altar and a scroll bearing the Japanese characters for "Light." Prayers before this and similar holy scrolls, regarded as Sacred Focal Points of God's Direct Light, are said to be especially effective. Some members have similar scrolls in their homes before which they say daily prayers.

I had come to the church for a conference with two of its ministers, one an American woman and the other a man from Japan. Afterward, the woman, formerly a medical technologist and now a full-time World Messianity minister, kindly asked me if I would like to receive Johrei. I consented.

As I sat in the chair facing the altar, the minister was seated facing me. After a silent prayer, she raised her hand. It was held with the back of the hand over the point between her eyebrows, the palm outward, slightly cupped like a concave lens, and aimed at me.

I waited in the still church, hands folded, as the palm curved over me from a distance of perhaps three feet. Other people in the church, both Japanese and Occidental, were also receiving Johrei—not necessarily from ministers, for any instructed member is empowered to bestow it. As the minutes passed, the woman's hand slowly moved to focus the Light on various parts of my body. After about five minutes, I was asked to turn around to receive Johrei on my back. Then, to turn forward again.

Whether it was from the power of Johrei, or from simply sitting very quietly in a holy place, this experience had an effect on me. That morning, beneath the surface, I had been worried about some personal and financial matters. Among other things, my wife and I had bought a fairly expensive steam iron the day before and had carelessly left it on a counter somewhere in the store. I had next to go there to see if it could be found.

As I sat for Johrei, I felt my mind lose consciousness of all these things. I felt not tedium but a sort of intense "eternal now" awareness of the church room—the color and texture of the wood, the glint of light from the rich scroll over the altar, the quiet movement of the other people coming and going from Johrei. A lighthearted inner joy, and a mild sense of warmth, arose within me.

Later, I found that a clerk had put the iron behind a counter and it had not been stolen, and all through the day good things happened that resolved the other problems over which I had been agitated.

Upon leaving, the minister told me that the vibrations she had felt in her hand while giving me Johrei indicated that the toxins were particularly heavy in the back of my neck—a condition very common among cerebral people! She graciously urged me to receive further Johrei.

II

This simple act, Johrei, has drawn many people to the Church of World Messianity. Like most of the Japanese New Religions, it puts strong emphasis on the healing of mind and body. However, it does not give diagnosis or treatment in a medical sense. The "toxins" or "clouds" of which it speaks are essentially spiritual, caused by unbridled emotions, desires, and attachments, though they may have physical ramifications.

Meishu-sama taught that Johrei is the act of channeling the Direct Light of God, which is now coming into the world in greater and greater strength. We are now, he said, at a critical point in the spiritual history of the world. An age of water, which was also a time of darkness, is giving place to an era of purifying fire and light, when the supernal powers will be close to man and earth will be turned into a splendid near-heaven. In preparation for this, World Messianity has constructed miniature "paradises" at two places in Japan: Hakone and Atami. A site for a third has been purchased in Kyoto.

I received more insight into these things upon visiting an American couple who have joined the Church of World Messianity. Middle-aged, he a businessman and she a nurse, they lived in an old, comfortable, rambling house not far from the ocean. There was nothing outwardly "counter-culture" about their life-style or appearance. They might have been any middle-aged couple with teen-age children, except for the unusual sense of energy and joyous vitality that emanated from them.

But the home is also what is called a Johrei Center, and when I arrived I was first invited to go into an upstairs room, where I received Johrei. I could not help noticing the books in this shrine room, which also served as a study. Here was shelf after shelf of tomes on Eastern religion, reincarnation, and especially Theosophy and one offshoot of it, the Alice Bailey teachings about the New Age and the return of the Christ.

When we began talking downstairs, I inquired if these books were indicative of a cognate teaching, or perhaps of a spiritual history. The latter was closer to it. Back in that heyday of conventional American religion, the 1950's, this couple had been active in an ordinary church, busy with its suppers and building programs. But underneath, questions, feelings, psychic experiences arose of which that church seemed not to take account. Together, they began a spiritual search of their own which ran through many things—the library was a record of it. It ended in

World Messianity. They first heard about the teachings of Meishu-sama from a friend in the Edgar Cayce movement. The groups of people interested in that famous Kentucky seer, who died in 1945, have long been clearinghouses of information about new psychic and spiritual movements.

One day back in the early '60s, while a friend who was a member of World Messianity was visiting, the husband received a serious bruise on the head. The friend asked if he would like to receive Johrei. In considerable pain, he agreed. He reports that as the Johrei was being channeled, the swelling visibly decreased and the pain vanished.

This, together with parallel experiences of watching the power of Johrei on other people with more serious ailments, convinced them that it was something special. They emphasize, of course, that Johrei is not "faith healing." Some psychics who practice "faith healing," in fact, reportedly receive Johrei regularly in order to keep up the inner purity necessary to their calling. Rather, it is believed to be the Direct Light of the New Age, the coming spiritual state of man, flowing in to purify the world, but also available to individuals.

People have to be purified, in fact, so that they can stay here when the paradise comes. The attractiveness of Johrei is simply its objectivity. A Johrei session does not require the verbal intimacy of confession or counseling, nor the physical intimacy of the laying on of hands; one is simply there, and to receive its blessing requires no particular emotions, but only openness.

Johrei, whose ultimate purpose is to purify, can be applied to all sorts of situations. I heard story after story of healings, the giving up of drug abuse, and conversion of life with the help of Johrei. I was even told that the accident rate at a certain freeway off-ramp had gone down dramatically after some World Messianity people had begun "Johrei-ing" it every time they passed by, and that this was confirmed by an amazed police department.

It was agreed that World Messianity spreads mostly by word of mouth. Probably most people are first drawn by accounts of the healing effectiveness of Johrei and come in desperation with physical or mental problems. Once these are taken care of, though, and the revitalized individual starts to look for a philosophy of life to go with his new self, other aspects of World Messianity may speak to him.

III

One of these is nature farming. Its fundamental concept is preserving "the natural vitality and fertility" of soil by not using any fertilizers or insecticides. Meishusama, who first publicly promoted nature farming in 1949, said, "Natural, pure soil is permeated with the spiritual energy of soil, which is the true growth or fertility factor." He added that the food grown in pure soil is full of the natural nutritional elements necessary for the body.

The use of artificial chemicals, he believed, actually encourages the prevalence of toxins and insects by lowering the spiritual energy of fields and crops. Nature farming differs from organic farming in that in the former not even biological fertilizers, such as manure, are used. It is believed that pure dirt alone is the only growth-giving agent; the farmer's real task is to keep the soil absolutely pure of any alien substance. Also contrary to the canons of scientific farming, it teaches that crops need not be rotated, but that growing the same crop in the same soil time after time habituates the soil to that plant and causes it to flourish better and better as the seasons go by.

On the other hand, the World Messianity nature farmer has working for him the powers of the incoming Light. Seeds and soil alike are given Johrei to purify them of any negative vibrations caused by previously applied impure chemicals and to give them energy for growth. The real secret behind nature farming is a return to an archaic sense of the farmer's relationship to his crops as one of reverence and spiritual unity, in which producing a harvest is an act of the gods, not of man alone. It recovers an agricultural world very different from that of scientific agronomy. However, it is of a piece with recent laboratory evidence that plants do respond to a positive psychic atmosphere—if you will, to prayer and telepathy and love—and go into shock conditions in the presence of violence and death.[21]

The world of nature farming is well epitomized in an account that appeared in several 1972 issues of a World Messianity paper of the experiences with it of two young American members, Jack and Nina Phalen of Boulder, Colorado. They encountered no small resistance in establishing their garden. The local citizens apparently disliked the couple's long-hair appearance and "counter-culture" life-style, though gentler people would be hard to imagine. About 1971, Jack and Nina managed to begin the project effectively. Here it is in Jack's own words:

> So, with Nina and myself, and two other people who own an herb shop here, we started. We started planting around the first of April, and everything was going very well, and of course I Johreied the seeds before we planted them. I usually did a handful at a time, although if you

could do a greater quantity at a time it would work the same. It just seemed like it was such a beautiful part of the blessing, to pour a handful of seeds into your hand and kneel and channel to them for 15 or 20 seconds—enough time to pray and to channel.

I would pray to God through Meishu-sama and the Church of World Messianity, and ask that the vibrations of the seeds be raised and they be blessed so they would grow into strong, healthy plants to provide enough food for many people. Then I would plant them—and they grew! As a matter of fact, we have almost 100% germination! One of our problems was trying to thin things—we will not make the same mistake next year. I'll plant seeds very sparsely if I have Johreied them first, because where there would usually be 70–80% germination, I was having at least 95%. . . .

When Reverend Dowd came to give the course and brought the Nature Farming information from Bruce Tuthill, he mentioned doing a special prayer for ladybugs if we needed them—and we did! So I tried it, and prayed to the Father, through Meishu-sama, and asked to be put in communication with the Deva of the spirit in control of bug life on the planet. Then I asked the spirit if he would send me as many ladybugs as he could spare! And we had so many ladybugs the owner of the property, who had been gardening for ten years, said there were at least twice as many as he had ever seen. There were ladybugs literally all over the garden, and they just ate up all the little aphids that were bothering the plants. . . .

If there was a special plant that you noticed needed Johrei, then you would go over and channel to it. We didn't really give the garden Johrei every day, but it gave the garden so much protection! It really did. I told you about the hailstorm. It was a horrible storm, just terrible. We were coming down from the mountains. . . . I had with me my little prayer book, and I thought, I'll just chant the Amatsu Norito and pray for protection for our garden. So I did, very quietly. . . .

Nothing had been harmed, though we heard stories of other people's gardens where they had been absolutely, totally ruined, right in the same area, completely flattened to the ground and everything ruined. And nothing had been hurt in ours! [22]

IV

The movement that has brought about the stopping of traffic accidents and the marvelous production of ladybugs began thousands of miles across the sea in the ministry of Mokichi Okada (1882–1955), or Meishu-sama, as he is now called.

Okada came of poor background. His father was a secondhand dealer with a road stall in Tokyo. Added to the young Okada's poverty was chronic sickness. As a young man, he tried a series of business ventures. Some of them were successful for a time, but reversals, illnesses, and nervous breakdowns due to overwork pursued him. Finally, when he was forty-two, he was completely ruined by the great earthquake of 1923.

Although in early life Okada had been an atheist, shortly before this time he began studying the teachings of the Omoto faith, with their emphasis on spirit communication and a New Age with a New Messiah. Following the earthquake disaster, Okada plunged himself into Omoto wholeheartedly.

This led to an experience in December 1926 when Okada was entered by a divine spirit, said to be a form of Kannon, the great Buddhist bodhisattva of mercy, always very popular in Japan. He told him he was to use his body to work for the salvation of mankind. Okada received the impression that he was the first human being brought into such total union with the Divine Source. He said that Kannon was using him unreservedly as his instrument. In a poem, he later wrote:

> I feel very strange
> When I think about myself,
> For I am a man,
> Yet not a man, since I am
> Used as God's instrument. . . .
>
> I have been chosen
> By God as His instrument
> And as His channel
> To save the world.
> I feel strange
> At thought of my destiny.[23]

He said that on this occasion he had also received the Direct Light of God, the Johrei light, which was to be dispensed into the world starting with his ministry.

At that time, Okada was told by his divine mentors to "prepare pencil and paper." Through spirit communications, dictated to his wife, he received the history of Japan for the period between 500,000 and 7,000 years ago, and also made future prophecies, which his followers say have all come true. The procedure was the same as that by which Onisaburo Deguchi of Omoto had received the many-volumed *Reikai Monogatari* ("Tales of the Spirit World") a few years before.

On June 15, 1931, Okada was inspired to climb a mountain called Nokogiri. There he recited a prayer called the Amatsu Norito. This prayer, he said, was the oldest and most powerful prayer in the world, and its sounds had mantic power. We have seen how Jack Phalen used it to divert a hailstorm. This prayer is very important in the public and private worship of World Messianity; it is re-

cited in Japanese at every service of worship, and in the
home in private prayers. In title, diction, and content it
is quite similar to a class of prayers that have been used
in Shinto worship since ancient times, although its word-
ing is not exactly identical to that of any known early
prayer; it is said that Meishu-sama made changes in the
pronunciation of words to increase their spiritual vibra-
tion. On that mountaintop Meishu-sama received the revelation which that day marked the dawning of the New
Age. Forty-one years later, seven prospective ministers of
World Messianity, including two Americans, climbed the
same mountain and recited the Amatsu Norito together.

During the years of his spiritual development, Okada
was related to Omoto as teacher, branch leader, and practitioner of its healing techniques. He joined Omoto in
1920, but was not active in it for long then. He renewed
his faith in 1924, and soon afterward two individuals, one
an Omoto member and one a nonmember, reported they
could see visions of Kannon over Meishu-sama's head. One
of these was a Mitsuo Azuma, who had previously received a prophecy in Manchuria that he would find a man
who could channel light. Okada himself was not sure what
these strange things meant, since he had not yet received
his call. But clearly he was set apart from the Omoto rank
and file.

After the 1926 and 1931 experiences, Okada went his
own way more and more. He experimented with various
methods of channeling the healing light, precursors of
modern Johrei practice. Finally, in 1934, he broke with
Omoto—fortunately, since shortly afterward the increasingly repressive government suppressed that faith.

The same year, a man came to see Okada, and before
leaving took a photograph of him. When the picture was

developed he was amazed to find a figure of Kannon above Okada's head. Copies of the picture were distributed to Okada's followers who wanted them.

One can see many parallels between the early Okada and the flamboyant Onisaburo Deguchi. Both reported dramatic initiatory experiences in which they were called to Messiahship as substitutes for God on earth. Deguchi said he incarnated Miroku, the coming Buddha of the future, while Okada, though he also emphasized Miroku, was the vehicle of Kannon. Deguchi dictated the *Reikai Monogatari*; Okada followed with his own spirit-written work, though many of his ideas closely resemble those of the Omoto scriptures. Omoto used in healing a paddle-shaped piece of wood inscribed with characters; Okada briefly employed a fan or piece of paper with "Light" written thereon.

In 1935, Okada established his own organization, the Dai Nihon Kannon Kai ("Japanese Kannon Association"). Kannon was then particularly important for Okada, and as we have seen was detected clairvoyantly to be associated with him. Okada said that according to his revelation Kannon had been revealed to him to be a divine spirit of the highest rank who belonged to the fire line. During the dark age of water, this mighty being had to work within Buddhism as a bodhisattva to help suffering humanity, taking countless forms and playing innumerable roles. But now that the New Age is advancing, he is taking a higher rank, as Komyo-nyorai ("Coming One of Light"), called Miroku in Buddhism or Messiah in the West, to work for the unfolding of God's plan.

After establishing the Kannon Association, Okada was making his entire living from his healing ministry and his teaching work. He was not a totally religious person in any solemn, exclusive manner, however. Okada loved the cinema and the theater, and went out in public with his wife when this was still a bit daring in Japan. He wrote verse and humorous prose, and even founded a society for humorous literature.

Okada used various means of healing, various ways of channeling the Johrei purifying light he believed he had received in 1926. He distributed pieces of a special paper with the character *hikari* ("Light") written on them—the "Sacred Focal Point" of today's World Messianity. This is a symbol worn by all members as a transmitter of the Divine Light. It is folded and placed in a small container made of pure white silk and worn around the neck. Every word has its own vibratory rate, and "Light," generated by the meeting of fire and water, has the highest and most auspicious rate of all.

Okada's independent healing work was successful, bringing him both wealth and fame. Distinguished people in the military and literary worlds were among his public supporters. But just after the new organization was founded, Okada was arrested and prosecuted for fraud and illegal practice of medicine. He could only resume his work as a licensed practitioner of folk medicine, without overt spiritual claims. The totalitarian nature of the government of those days, which was also putting extreme pressure on Christianity and other minority beliefs, should be taken into account in evaluating the incident.

During the Second World War a faithful band of disciples remained close to Okada. It is said that he predicted the war, Japan's defeat, and the great postwar social changes, and that during the war he shared with his followers prophecies that were most helpful in those difficult times. Okada warned his people to leave Tokyo before the terrible fire-bombings began. The leader himself moved to Atami. On one occasion he told a young man notified to report for the draft not to worry about it—and it turned out he was to report on August 15, 1945, the day the war ended.

Okada assured his band that the dreadful agony that Japan and the world was undergoing was part of the purifying fire scouring earth in preparation for the New Age. Followers said afterward they were spared from bombings by wearing the "Sacred Focal Point." Many healings by Johrei methods, including healings of victims of the atomic bomb at Hiroshima, were told of in the aftermath of the war.

It might be pointed out here that, while much is made in World Messianity of accounts of events that seem miraculous, for believers this is not just credulous wondermongering or an indication of selfish desire for personal benefit. The motives of human beings no doubt are always mixed. But World Messianity teachers stipulate that the real meaning of the miraculous today is what it was in New Testament times—a *sign*. Miracles of protection and healing, and the presence in our century of men and means of apparent supernormal power, are pointers that a God who lives and acts, and who is causing an old age to pass away as a new and far better one supersedes it, is at work on the face of old earth. The miracles of Johrei are foretastes of the Light that is coming into the world. At the same time, World Messianity today strongly emphasizes that Johrei is not intended to take the place of medical treatment, and that "channels" should stringently avoid any such use of it or even casual words that might tend to imply that it is.

Okada emerged from the bitter fires of the war tested,

deepened, and stabilized as a spiritual leader. While certainly his earlier stages of call, experimentation, and slow separation from the ways of Omoto were not repudiated, there is something about the postwar Okada which is profounder, having been refined through great trials and deep reflection. He is now a man ready to enter upon the major phase of his work. He is more independent. He can leave behind Omoto spiritualism, and strike out in new directions. He is more universal in his vision, able to relate his work to the Christian as well as the Buddhist and Shinto traditions. The dark valley of the war and the increasing pressure of the Light have made him more impassioned with his greatest theme: the time of troubles and the coming transformation of the entire world, through his purifying Light, into paradise.

In 1947, thanks to the new religious freedom, he was able to reactivate his organization as the Nihon Kannon Kyodan ("Japanese Kannon Church"). In 1948 he also started a Nihon Miroku Kyokai ("Japanese Miroku Church"). Miroku is Maitreya, the coming Buddha of the future, and as we have seen for Okada the new messianic form of the same great being called also Kannon.

His labors greatly prospered in the free atmosphere of postwar Japan. In 1950 the two groups were combined into the Sekai Meshiya Kyo or Sekai Kyusei Kyo, officially called in English the Church of World Messianity. It is from the Hebrew "Messiah"—coming, expected Savior. "Messiah" is of course the title of Jesus Christ, and of he whom the Jews still expect. Messiah means literally "the anointed one," and *christos* is a literal Greek translation of it, so "messianity" really means the same thing as Christianity. But Okada meant the word to be future-oriented —to look toward the impending coming of a *real* messianic age, when the paradise that Christians expect at the Second Coming of Christ will be imminently brought into being as the glorious weight of the Light increases.

Two motifs are evident in this change of terminology: the dropping of the name "Japan" in the title in favor of "world," and the abandoning of the Buddhist names in favor of one with strong Judeo-Christian overtones, and with even more powerful eschatological, or future savior and world-transformation, suggestiveness.

By 1950 the movement had grown from a handful to over 300,000 followers. With the new organization, the movement's emphases were rapidly moving toward their present shape. It was more and more stressed that Johrei is a channeling of spiritual light as well as a means of physical healing. The movement was presented as being an instrument for the spiritual uniting of East and West. Nature farming appeared in 1949.

As World Messianity became more affluent, Okada was able to demonstrate its ultimate meaning by developing extensive miniature paradises, foresamples of the New Age. One was built in Atami, and another in Hakone, both beautiful resort cities. The paradises, with their art museums and azalea gardens and sanctuaries, exemplified a major point of World Messianity: consciousness of beauty.

However, in the early 1950's troubles also befell the movement. In 1950 a great fire swept through Atami, but stopped just at the gates of the World Messianity headquarters, a fact the faithful interpreted as a miraculous sign. Later in 1950, Okada was arrested and convicted of tax evasion and graft. In order to avoid further legal controversy, he paid a fine. World Messianity people say that no deliberate fraud was involved on Okada's part, but that he was concerned with spiritual matters rather than the church's financial business, which were fouled by a loose, inaccurate bookkeeping system and an incompetent secretary. They also suggest that religious persecution was involved.

Then, in 1954, the leader fainted and fell after several days of intense work. Thereafter his health failed, and on February 9, 1955, after refusing medical attention, he died.

Some of the early membership fell away as the controversial, colorful, and unforgettable Okada was succeeded in the leadership by his widow, who was called Nidai-sama, "The Second Generation." She said that she received guidance from the departed founder, now regarded as the supreme heavenly intercessor and called Meishu-sama. Under Nidai-sama's leadership, the faith moved more and more away from a primary healing emphasis to its task of world redemption through the channeling of the Light. It was back on a course of growth when in 1962 Nidai-sama was succeeded by her daughter Itsuki, called Sandai-sama or Kyoshu-sama.

Building continued. A sanctuary was completed in Atami under Nidai-sama, a structure said to symbolize the coming together of East and West. In Kyoto a school and a training center have recently been opened. They are intended for new projects that will bring the church and society closer together. There is a center for research work in environmental science, on nature farming and food, and on conventional treatment of physical problems. The presence of a clinic and a doctor represents a certain change in attitude. The center also houses a school of education.

In 1973 a dramatic reorganization of the church, in connection with a program of shift in emphasis and spiritual rejuvenation, transformed the church in Japan. It was said that some ministers were not on a sufficiently high level

of spiritual development and that confusion had crept into
the teaching. All churches were unified into forty-three,
one in each prefecture or major island. All ministers in
Japan were reassigned. Word went out that the emphasis
was now to be on spiritual joy, not on physical results,
and that in giving Johrei, stress was to be put on a prayer-
ful attitude, and little or none on the physical points in
the body. As we shall see, this shift is the culmination of
a long-standing trend and is attributed to the results of
the continuing increase in the incoming of the Light. The
reorganization did not affect the work in the United States,
except that some books are being rewritten to conform to
the new emphases.

V

World Messianity began on American soil on February
12, 1953. On that day a minister, the Reverend Kiyoko
Higuchi, arrived in Honolulu. This attractive and remarkable woman has certainly been the main force in the
bringing of World Messianity to America. More recently
she has been engaged in translation work, and has Eng-
lished most of the fundamental World Messianity teachings.

Formal work on mainland America was started in 1954.
While in Hawaii, Ms. Higuchi had been traveling back
and forth to California and laid the foundation for the
work there. The Los Angeles church was incorporated
and chartered in 1954. In December of 1955 she moved
from Hawaii to Los Angeles in order to concentrate all her
energies on the mainland.

In 1967 an old Armenian church building was purchased
in Los Angeles. It is a spacious edifice, befitting the present large Japanese and Occidental congregation.

Another project of the late 1950's and the 1960's was the establishing of a center in Valley Center, California, opened in June, 1958. The plan was to make it the site of the first miniature paradise in America. Fruits and vegetables were grown at this center by the nature farming method. However, the church came to the conclusion in the early 1970's that the project was premature. Plans were made to sell the land, and make a search for a more appropriate site.

The first Occidental couple were Mr. and Mrs. Ivan Buster, who joined the church in Hawaii in 1953 and later moved to San Francisco. A noticeable growth among Occidentals began in 1956. In 1969, young people with a background in the "hippie" life-style started to join the church. By 1974 their numbers reached at least 500. Some found that Johrei helped them to stop using drugs. This growth was located particularly in the San Francisco area and around Boulder, Colorado.

A few older Americans who had entered the church have been especially helpful in providing wise guidance and sponsorship to the younger people. There is the couple already mentioned; their home has become a real haven for young people, many of them with serious problems. Here they have been able to talk, and to receive Johrei if they wish. The American minister who gave me Johrei makes frequent trips to Boulder to be with the mostly young World Messianity community there. Both of these works are indirect advertisements of the peculiar, perhaps unexpected, power of this Japanese spiritual movement to answer the spiritual quest many of them are embarked upon, or to assuage their troubles.

A word should be said about the frequent and well-organized pilgrimages that the American members, Japanese-American and Occidental, make to Japan, usually on the occasion of the opening of a new building or a major celebration there. These events are naturally exciting and deeply meaningful to the members on the outskirts of the church's extension. American churches and centers will hear reports and see slides and movies of the journey and of the welcome, warm and impressive as only the Japanese can manage, they received. Needless to say, these trans-pacific flights do much to consolidate loyalty in American members and reconvince them of the movement's importance.

VI

The present doctrinal teaching of the Church of World Messianity, implicit in Meishu-sama's work from the beginning, centers around belief that revelation was given to Meishu-sama concerning the coming New Age, and that God's Direct Light, long kept in abeyance, is now being released into the world starting from his ministry. The Light began to move in the highest point of heaven in 1881, reached the etheric plane in 1931, and is now intensifying within the ordinary world itself. We are now in a period of critical and cataclysmic change. But these trials are the birth pangs of a new era, the Kingdom of God. Their final end will be the creation of a paradise on earth, a world freed from all poverty, disease, and conflict. The present times are the transitional period from the Old Age to the New, what is called the Messianic Age by many Jews, the Last Judgment by Christians. The purifying Light—Johrei—is the means of cleansing the world to clear the way for paradise. The Church of World Messianity's work is thus of crucial importance, though it is not said to be the only means God is using or has used. Meishu-sama once wrote in verse:

> The world's tottering
> Like a high-piled stack of eggs.
> When it comes crashing,
> How can any man be saved
> Except by praying to God? [24]

The Church of World Messianity teaches three principles in its task of paradise-world preparation, often called the Divine Light Program: Johrei, nature farming, and consciousness of beauty.

Johrei prepares for paradise by channeling the cleansing Light to remove clouds, or negative vibrations, from the individual's spiritual body. As a result, toxins in the physical body often dissolve and are eliminated so that physical purification can take place.

Nature farming is a way of cleansing the earth itself. It restores the earth and prepares it to bear upon its bosom a paradise for all life. It makes pure the soil; and soil, water, and fire are the three basic elements in Meishu-sama's system.

Consciousness of beauty is revealed preeminently in the miniature paradises in Japan. Meishu-sama liked to say that "religion is the mother of art." It is also said that divine administration is worked out in accordance with patterns; if a divine pattern is established at one place, as day follows night it will be duplicated elsewhere, until ultimately it enwraps the whole earth. Recently a flower arrangement school following Meishu-sama's style was opened at the Mother Church in Atami; this is regarded as an extremely significant development. Experiencing beauty in itself is like Johrei in that it purifies one from clouds, raising one spiritually to a higher plane.

Undoubtedly the construction of the paradises was one of the major factors in the postwar success of World Messianity. There is something especially Japanese, and also profoundly humanistic, about regarding a landscaped garden, in which nature and the works of man are united in an aesthetic vision, as a supreme work of art, and perhaps the art form that is most deeply meaningful as a preview of a potentially paradisal future. We in the West have tended to feel that nature must be either completely "conquered" or else left completely intact as wilderness. But Meishu-sama's garden paradises both exemplified a creative synthesis of Eastern and Western visions of the relation of man to nature and helped restore to postwar Japan confidence in its own cultural heritage.

Underlying all these principles is obviously a dualistic view of man's milieu: everything is conceptualized in terms of purity versus "clouds" or "toxins."

Behind this, as one might expect, is a dualistic metaphysical system. First, there is the principle of the spiritual world. Meishu-sama starts with the premise that the cosmos contains two worlds, the physical and the spiritual. In the past, he tells us, the physical world has been the primary focus of mankind's interest and efforts, since the other cannot be perceived by ordinary means. But the spiritual world is actually primary, the cause of the physical.

The causative spiritual world is a complex system. World Messianity must be especially attractive to people who, like Meishu-sama, think of spiritual realities in picture terms, for it continually uses spatial and imagistic metaphors: planes, light, cords, and the like.

At the summit is God, who is *kakuremi*, a "hidden be-ing." First before him are ranged the great spirits, no longer in the physical body, who work for him in the oper-ation of the cosmos—they are those called angels, bodhi-sattvas, devas, kami, and so forth in the various religions. Next dwell the spirits of the departed from earth, high and low, each on its appropriate plane.

Then, also before God, is the Yukon (literally, "mystic soul" or perhaps "numinous soul") of each individual on earth. Each person has a Yukon as a sort of representative or archetype of himself in the spiritual realm. Its rising and falling is a barometer of the individual's progress to-ward purity. It also is a means of communication between God and the individual, for each Yukon is connected, as it were by a telegraph wire, to its respective person on this planet.

Finally, each person here has a spiritual body, coexten-sive with his physical shape, which is susceptible to good or bad spiritual influences—for not all that is in the spir-itual world is wholesome.

To complete the picture we must see this whole spir-itual world, at least as it relates to earth, as now in a state of great excitement and upheaval with the increasing pres-sure of the Direct Light.

Meishu-sama says it is almost impossible for the ordi-nary individual to make intuitive contact with his Yukon. That can be done only after some degree of spiritual puri-fication. This purification also affects the status of one's Yukon above. If one's Yukon is on a high plane, its state is reflected in one's physical life. For example, Meishu-sama tells us that

> one whose Yukon is on a higher plane in the spiritual
> realm will be led to a desirable location when searching

for another home. He will go to the right house quite naturally, or, if building a new one, will be guided in making the plans. One whose Yukon is low will be led to a location and a house corresponding to that level.[25]

Not only is one's spiritual body connected with his Yukon and with God; they are also connected with each other, by means of the "spiritual cord." Meishu-sama describes the cords in a typically very imagistic way:

> Many people seem to be unfamiliar with the term "spiritual cord," probably because the existence of the cord itself is not generally known. While the spiritual cord is invisible, being of exceedingly fine texture—finer than atmosphere—its role and influence in physical life are so great it cannot be lightly regarded. The cord is the conveyor of life-supporting energies, and it influences the fate of human beings and even the world's destiny at large. . . .
>
> There are innumerable invisible cords connecting you with the people around you—hundreds, thousands of them. Some are large and some are small, some are long and some are short, some are bright and some are dull.[26]

Meishu-sama goes on to say that the largest cord is that between husband and wife, and that next in size is that between parent and child, and so on.

A related concept is that of the aura. As in Western occultism, the aura is described by Meishu-sama as being a light that can be seen by clairvoyants and emanates around a person from the spiritual body through the physical body. Its color, brilliance, and width are indicators of spiritual and physical health. Following the rule that the spiritual world is causative to the physical, these facts can have consequence in the material world. For example:

> If an individual has a wide aura, the spirit of an automobile (*everything* has a spirit) cannot hit him because

of the strength of his aura. The physical automobile will turn aside and the individual will be safe.[27]

In this spiritual-physical world, man lives a life of freedom of choice. He has really two spiritual natures, the primary, which is an individualized part of God and therefore divine, and the animalistic secondary spirit, which is at odds with it. Both are in contact with outside helpful or baneful spiritual forces—the primary with a guardian spirit, selected from among the person's ancestors, and the secondary with evil spirits. (Here, in the two souls, and in the concept of a guardian ancestral spirit, we see Oriental influence enter a system that otherwise closely parallels Western spiritualism.) Meishu-sama also speaks of three spirits in a person: primary, secondary, and guardian. As the power of the secondary spirit waxes, "clouds" and "toxins" increase and must be purified away by suffering, service, prayers, beauty, and receiving and channeling Johrei. The "clouds" are really thought forms, desires, emotions, and attachments, characteristically objectified as dark bodies which clog up free flow to the spiritual world of the Yukon and the higher realm of God.

The concept of life after death combines spiritualism and reincarnation. A person lived in the spiritual world before birth, and after death he passes to it again, entering a plane that corresponds to his degree of purity. After he is purified, tens, hundreds, or thousands of years later, he returns to earth to take a physical body again. Some unfortunate people, however, have such a strong attachment to earth that they are drawn back to be reincarnate before their time, when they still bear with them much impurity. These people will suffer greatly, and also perhaps cause much trouble, in the world.

The spiritual world is now, as a result of the influx of

the New Age Light, in a state of disruption. Mediumistic communication with spirits is not encouraged by World Messianity, but is said to happen sometimes. Especially when a person is undergoing Johrei, he may be seized by a spirit, more likely than not ancestral, who is confused by what is going on. The spirit will have to be purified too. The chaotic activity of evil spirits is more frenzied now than ever, for they sense the incoming of the Light and the nearness of their ruin.

VII

The practical means which the Church of World Messianity uses in its service of the Light, apart from large-scale works such as the paradises and nature farming, and general vehicles such as education and charity, may be summarized as follows: (1) Johrei, (2) the Sacred Scroll bearing the character *komyo*, "Light," which hangs in every church and home shrine, (3) the Sacred Focal Point, the slip of paper with the character *hikari*, "Light," worn around the neck, and (4) the powerful Amatsu Norito.

These themes are evident in the major services of worship. On June 18, 1972, I attended the service of the festival called Recognition Day of Paradise on Earth at the Los Angeles church. The church was crowded, for delegations had come from all over California for this high service. It is in commemoration of the "dawning of the New Age in the spiritual realm beginning on June 15, 1931, as revealed to Meishu-sama," the same occasion when he received his revelation concerning the New Age while reciting the Amatsu Norito.

The Los Angeles church was a natural place for this service, for it is the only place of worship designated a "church" on the mainland of the United States. The other major centers—San Francisco, Long Beach, San Jose, Salt Lake City, Boulder, and others—meet mostly in private homes, and are called "Johrei Centers." The Los Angeles church, of which all mainland U.S. World Messianity people are nominal members, is governed by a Board of Trustees, comprised of six ministers and six lay members, half of whom are Occidentals, plus the head minister, who is the president of the corporation. At the present time ministers undergo no formal training program (both in Japan and America, training is on a personal, *ad hoc* basis), but a training institute is now being set up in Japan. The ministers are all appointed from Japan by the International Division of the headquarters. While the worldwide church is under the leadership of Kyoshu-sama, daughter of Mokichi Okada, her direction is generally restricted to spiritual matters. The administrative head is Teruaki Kawai, Socho or Supervising Minister, who was appointed by Kyoshu-sama from among the Board of Directors elected by all male members. The Board of Trustees of the Los Angeles church, which handles the church's temporalities, was elected by a Board of Representatives, which in turn was elected by the congregation.

After an organ prelude, the service opened with prayers in English and Japanese said by a minister standing in formal posture before the Sacred Scroll with the inscription *komyo* written on it.

Next, also toward the Sacred Scroll, the Amatsu Norito and the Lord's Prayer were said in unison. The Lord's Prayer is an addition of the church in America; it is not used in World Messianity services in Japan. The Amatsu Norito, which is supposed to be essentially *kotodama*, words whose effect, like that of a Hindu or Buddhist mantram, comes just from the vibrations of their sounds rather than from their meaning, begins with a prayer for purification. It goes on to a characteristically Shinto invocation of the "*ama-tsu-kami, kuni-tsu-kami*," the gods of heaven and the gods of earth (for Meishu-sama, identical with the higher denizens of the spiritual world), and ends with petitions (apparently added later) to Miroku and the deified founder Meishu-sama himself to "protect and prosper us." It is typical of Oriental religion that it deifies and prays to spiritual leaders far more readily than Western —except in the case of Jesus Christ, and in a different sense the saints of Catholicism and Orthodoxy. Finally the prayer asks that our souls may shine like gods (literally, like the kami or angelic spirit beings, or like Miroku, the great deity of the New Age).

The Amatsu Norito was followed by a chanting of poems for Recognition Day. Then Johrei was given to the entire congregation by the beloved lady who had first brought World Messianity to the United States nearly twenty years before. Holding her hand near her face, she moved it slowly over the assembly for about fifteen minutes.

Sermons were given in English and Japanese. The English address was by the Reverend Thelma Dowd, the same minister who first gave me Johrei. It began with a brief summary of World Messianity history and teaching. She emphasized the emergence of ten-year cycles in the story of the church, beginning with the Light's "reaching the etheric plane" in 1931, and pointed to a new decade just opening now. On a larger scale, she spoke of the ending of the age of water in the language of Western astrology, talking of the passing of the Piscean Age and the incoming of the Aquarian.

The new decade is to be one of great openness on the

part of the Church of World Messianity, and of wider involvement in the problems of humanity. Ms. Dowd quoted from a recent address by the Reverend Teruaki Kawai, Supervising Minister of the worldwide church:

> Because of its self-protective attitude up to the present, the church has had a somewhat closed attitude, and therefore it tended to have a negative vibration. We wish now to create a more open and positive atmosphere. It is not in harmony with Meishu-sama's wish to remain alienated from society by being closed in within a rigid framework of religion, by building a fortress called the Church of World Messianity. However loudly we may say Meishu-sama was a wonderful person, or World Messianity is an outstanding religion, it means nothing if the public in general does not recognize and accept them. In order to gain this recognition and acceptance, we wish now to go out into society with our most positive attitude.

In evidence of the new attitude, three new activities were adduced: new projects in nature farming and work on problems of environmental science and pollution; the flower arrangement school; and the new training institute for leaders, designed to make them whole and complete persons. Greater emphasis on education is typical of the second generation of most religious movements, when the transition from charismatic to rational, routinized leadership must be made.

Yet the role of accounts of marvelous healing was not lost. The sermon ended with two or three of them. One was of an elderly Japanese-American woman who had lost a malignant growth from her mouth after receiving Johrei. The woman herself was present, and she proudly processed up and down the aisles of the church, showing the extracted growth, neatly taped to a large cardboard, to the whole congregation.

The service continued with solos by a long-haired member of Occidental descent. Announcements followed the benediction. At once we were brought into the world of the Church of World Messianity as a concrete sociological entity in modern California. The delegates, predominantly Japanese-Americans from various communities from Sacramento to San Diego, were introduced and applauded, as were those who had sung or played during the service. We were told that a visit by leaders from Japan was temporarily canceled because more urgent matters in Brazil required their attention.

A carnival to be held by the church in August was discussed. Although fast dying out as a means of raising funds in most American churches, carnivals are a staple of Japanese-American religious groups, whether Buddhist, Christian, or New Religions. These are very elaborate events, requiring months of extensive planning. They are opportunities for wide segments of the Japanese-American community to meet each other, eat Japanese food, and support the various faiths of that religiously remarkably diverse, but also remarkably tolerant and commonsensical, community.

VIII

It was evident that the Church of World Messianity in America consists of two congregations, the Japanese-American and the Occidental. The life-style contrast is sharp. The Japanese-American followers of Meishu-sama were, by and large, not young, and showed a neat, white-shirt-and-tie dignity and conservatism of manner that is

overwhelmingly characteristic of Japanese-American society as a whole.

The Occidentals run mostly to (a) middle-aged people
whose dress is not out of the ordinary but who have about
them an air of long preoccupation with mysticism, astrology, theosophy, and the like; and (b) young people with
long hair and pioneer-length print dresses, the sort who
immediately suggest, not drugs, but guitars, hitchhiking,
and health-food diets.

It is a tribute to the Church of World Messianity that
it is able to hold together in apparent mutual respect two
such disparate worlds. Much of the credit belongs to
Western ministers and older couples who are not themselves counter-culture. But, perhaps out of their own unorthodox spiritual quest years before such ventures were
fashionable, they are the rare sort of older persons with
whom the alienated young feel they can communicate.
They radiate to them sincerity, openness, a sense that they
care, and enthusiasm over a spiritual discovery. And everyone who is sincere wants to know about a spiritual discovery that really works and engenders joyful enthusiasm.

People like these, and then the young people themselves, have made World Messianity and Johrei an "underground" spiritual force. They speak the same language as
other religious movements of the late 1960's. They talk of
a coming "Aquarian" age of paradise on earth, which explains the present time of terrible moving and shaking in
the historical and spiritual realms alike. They introduce
a simple spiritual technique which both objectifies spiritual transformation in one's inward life and makes it
"feelable." They find World Messianity compatible in concept with Occidental "esoteric" movements of long standing of the theosophical and spiritualistic sorts, as well as

with the Hindu movements in vogue in the same "underground" culture. Some World Messianity Occidental members, for example, apparently are both in it and in the Guru Maharaj Ji movement centering on that teen-age guru who has visited America recently. But they say that Maharaj Ji "knows what World Messianity is."

To join World Messianity one must first talk with a minister, then attend a course of six lectures, given according to a flexible schedule, which costs twenty-five dollars for the series. One is expected to have received Johrei five to ten times prior to the course, and every day during it. At the end of the course, one is united to the church in a brief service consisting of the Amatsu Norito and the Lord's Prayer. He is presented with the "Sacred Focal Point," the paper with *hikari*, "Light," inscribed on it, which is worn over his chest. He can now administer Johrei, though he will receive further guidance in its use. The church holds Johrei seminars, at which practitioners discuss the vibrations in their hands which various physical and mental problems in subjects induce and their interpretations.

Members pay six dollars a year in dues, and generally make a donation in a special envelope when receiving Johrei. They are expected to pray regularly, properly the Amatsu Norito and the Lord's Prayer, recited before a Sacred Scroll. I am told that some Occidentals do not care for the Amatsu Norito with its (to them) bizarre and meaningless collection of words, never fully translated into either English or modern Japanese, and with the seeming sorcery of putting faith just in its sounds. But others find its mantic tones stirring and marvelously effective, and commit it to memory.

Members are expected to give Johrei as often as possible, to people, animals (I have heard remarkable stories of its power to heal and calm beasts), seeds, and chancy situations. Basically Johrei is a means of letting the Direct Light into the world. Channels say that they can feel the vibrations becoming more and more intense with the passing years—today fifteen minutes of Johrei is as effective as an hour's a decade ago.

Apart from preferring food grown by nature farming, World Messianity takes a moderate attitude toward diet, smoking, and drinking. More important than rigid principles in these matters is not getting caught up in extremes of abstinence or indulgence, or in fads and fancies. The ideal is an open, balanced, tranquil, and ordered life.

The faith does not generally advertise, holding that a truly spiritual movement can spread only by word of mouth, or, rather, by its own divine means. However, its members are willing to talk about it, and its recent growth has been due mainly to enthusiastic rumor. It has grown out of experiences that individuals have had with Johrei, then spread to zeal for actively preparing for paradise on earth. The concept of the meeting of East and West, so deeply meaningful an idea to so many moderns, is very attractive.

Using the Japanese terms for Mahayana and Hinayana (Theravada) Buddhism (*Daijo* and *Shojo,* which words also connote in Japanese simply broad-mindedness and narrow-mindedness respectively), but applying them in a new way, Meishu-sama said that Western culture is *daijo,* broad, and Eastern is *shojo,* narrow, vertically oriented, "high and deep." What is needed is an *izunome,* a balanced cross, made of this horizontal and this vertical. Such a unified and completed and perfected world is the goal of the Church of World Messianity as it spans the Pacific.

READING SELECTION

*In the following passage from his writings, entitled
"Faith Works Miracles," Meishu-sama explains the sense
of being caught up in a time of wonder and change and
keen, believing hope which is so much a part of the World
Messianity experience.*

Throughout the known history of mankind, written records attest to the fact that faith and miracles are inseparably related. A religion in which no miracles ever occur cannot be called a true religion. However beautiful and elaborate its rituals may be, it has no value as a religion if its followers never experience miracles.

It is God Who performs miracles, not man. When an overwhelming blessing or a wondrous response to prayer is experienced, the event is generally considered a miracle. Through this kind of action, a person is moved to feel deep, reverent gratitude and a faith so strong he is protected from misfortune. By having such an experience he learns the priceless value of true faith. One personal experience is worth a hundred theories.

It is a matter of deep concern that not only has social evil abruptly increased, but also that the general trend of thought of the younger generation, the driving force of the future, is in utter confusion because of the bad influence of unwholesome ideas. I am convinced that overemphasis on materialistic education is responsible for this tragic condition. The problems of demoralization and juvenile delinquency will never be solved unless people are awakened to this great distortion.

In order to remove the worship of materialism, spiritual awareness must be aroused. But how can this be done? The only way is to awaken one and all to the reality of God, which nothing short of a miracle can accomplish. If the unbelievers see a seeming impossibility taking place before their very eyes, something beyond material explanation, all doubt and skepticism will vanish.

World-wide peace and the establishment of a sound, virtuous society can be achieved only when all people come to believe in the Existence of God through experiencing His miracle-working Power and a spiritual culture becomes a reality.

In this period of the great transition, God is releasing His Divine Holy Light for us. And such an intense, magnificent Light it is, performing one miracle after another! Never before in history have mortals been so blessed.

According to the revelation I received, God is releasing His Direct Light for the express purpose of awakening human minds, minds that are unaware of His Existence, minds that cannot even imagine His paradise on earth.

The one, omnipotent God, Who has worked through the great masters and teachers of all time, now directly shares His Light with all, to see man through this major transitional period.

Thus, by the miracles performed through the Divine Light, God's Plan for rescuing mankind from its own fallacies can be fulfilled. By His almighty Power, He will manifest more and more miraculous works.

Since miracles fit within the sphere of faith, we may well say, "Faith works miracles."

—*Teachings of Meishu-sama*, Vol. I,
Rev. ed. (Atami, Japan: Church
of World Messianity, 1965),
pp. 14–15.

5

Seicho-no-Ie,
*   The House of Growth*

I

I once attended a Seicho-no-Ie meeting at an old stucco
house done in moderately Spanish style on a quiet street
in Los Angeles. The inhabitants were a retired optometrist
and his wife who had lived in this residence for several
decades. The cool, dark interior, rich with overstuffed
furniture, Oriental carpets, books, and momentos of many
cultures, told me that this was one of those houses which
will be deathless in the memories of many who have been
inside it. A home like this is an inseparable extension of
the personalities who have long dwelt there, and in every
well-expressed human life there is something immortal.

A bright Chinese temple gong stood before the fireplace.
A hanging scroll of the great bodhisattva Kwan-yin (Kannon) ornamented a wall. Against another wall, a low book-
case was burdened with fat books on Ajurveda, the ancient
Indian system of medicine. On the second floor, the gentle
old doctor showed me his study, clearly the sanctuary of
a long-time pursuer of esoteric spiritual lore. Here were
fascinating shelves of books on theosophy, the arcane
reaches of yoga, the hidden teachings of Persia and Tibet.
A photograph of the Himalayas hung beside a window
open to a splendid vista of the glittering Los Angeles

basin. Religious images and artifacts from India and China decorated the walls. On the desk lay cards for the study of Arabic letters and Chinese characters. An ingenious home-made electrical device moved the letters of the Japanese syllabary one by one into view in a little window cut in a black cylinder for memorization. The doctor proudly showed me certificates of accomplishment in the Chinese exercise art of T'ai Chi Ch'uan. In an adjacent room, an elaborate display of bottles and jars, test tubes and retorts replete with multicolored powders and extracts brought to mind, in the castlelike atmosphere of this tower room, an old alchemist's laboratory.

Yet, while he had by no means given up interest in the secret lore of India, for the past nine years the optome-trist's main spiritual concern had been Seicho-no-Ie, a new Japanese movement centering around the teachings of Masaharu Taniguchi. As with other of the new reli-gions, many people from the West attracted to it have had a background as seekers within the esoteric, theosophical, and Oriental worlds.

The doctor said he had first learned about Seicho-no-Ie through a Japanese friend. He began attending meetings, which were then held in an upper room in a decrepit sec-tion of the city, but a place that many longtime Seicho-no-Ie people recall with nostalgia, despite the present beautiful and modernesque church.

He says that what was most attractive about Seicho-no-Ie was the way it affected him. It was not at first the ideas. Since the earlier meetings were in Japanese he could un-derstand little of them, but he could appreciate the charged spiritual atmosphere. In particular, the medita-tion method called shinsokan taught by Seicho-no-Ie seemed to impart a tangible power. He attributes healing and even the continuation of his life itself to its effect.

Seicho-no-Ie is a healing religion, and puts great emphasis on the power of thought to heal the physical body. But its real foundation is its metaphysical affirmation that everything is a manifestation of God and is perfect. The four basic principles of Seicho-no-Ie, the doctor said, are: (1) one truth, one God, one religion; (2) man a child of God; (3) reconciliation to everything in the universe; (4) gratitude to everybody and everything.

In other words, truth is God and therefore is one. Mind, thought, or consciousness is prior to the conditioned reality of everything in the phenomenal world, and at the heart of all thought is the divine within everyone. This means that all religions are basically expressions of awareness of this divine quality, and so the same. One must be accepting of this universal reality, since in itself it is perfect and its expressions are perfect; only dark thoughts in our own minds cloud recognition of this perfection. The Seicho-no-Ie way of opening oneself up to perfection is through feelings of gratitude. One of the most characteristic things about Seicho-no-Ie people and their meetings is their continual saying "Thank you very much," or the Japanese equivalent, "*Arigato gozaimasu*," to everyone and on every occasion.

The Seicho-no-Ie meetings, held in the doctor's house twice monthly, were the first English-speaking meetings in America. They are not completely English-speaking, since some chants and readings are still done in Japanese, it being believed that English is not conducive to the mantic Japanese thought forms that must be built up. When I attended in the autumn of 1972, about fifteen people were present, roughly half Oriental and half Occidental.

The meeting began with informal introductions, in which each person told who he was, where he lived, and something he liked to do. This group consisted of almost all middle-aged or elderly persons, and it was interesting that most said what he or she liked to do was listen to music. Nearly all also made a special point of expressing appreciation of the teachings of Masaharu Taniguchi.

After a couple minutes of silence and a hymn written by Taniguchi, sung in Japanese but to a Western tune, there followed an intriguing Seicho-no-Ie exercise called "laughing practice." After instructions by the leader, a personable youngish Japanese-American, everyone stood, put his hands on his belly, leaned back, and laughed heartily. Just watching the others deliberately trying to laugh was enough to send cascades of mirth around the room. "Laughing practice" certainly left the group in a relaxed, well-disposed frame of mind.

Next followed a long period of chanting the words *Jisso enman kanzen*, "Reality is absolutely perfect," over and over and over again to a fast, steady beat, until virtually a hypnotic euphoria had been set up.

Two or three short talks came next. An elderly American lady of Scottish descent described a recent trip to Scotland and the strange sequence of events that led to her seeing her family's ancestral castle. The optometrist read an account of a journey by astral traveling (whether his own or someone else's being ambiguous), in which the enraptured one saw the splendor and beauty of our entire world, and then was told by a mighty spirit he must return to this world and work in it for its purification. Finally, the young, practical-minded lay leader of the group, who clearly had some education both in Seicho-

no-Ie and in chemistry, rose to speak. He had brought
with him as a demonstration a box covered with clear
plastic containing four dice. He asked everyone to try
shaking it to turn up four of the same number. When no
one succeeded, he said the chances were only one in something like seven thousand. But this is nothing, he went on,
compared to the likelihood of the long, complex amino
acid and protein molecules upon which life is based coming into being through chance. To make biochemical molecules, hundreds of atoms must be arranged just right. That
virtually established the existence of a divine intelligence
behind the creation of life.

This talk was followed by reading aloud together, first
in English and then rapidly in Japanese with the intona-
tions of Buddhist sutra reading, the *Holy Sutra, Nectarean
Shower of Holy Doctrine*, of Taniguchi. Two long chapters, "God" and "Man," were recited; they were thick with
lines like these: "God, who is the creator of the whole universe, is beyond the five corporeal senses, even beyond the
sixth spiritual sense of human beings; Holy, Consummate,
Infinite . . ."

The session ended with the most important of all Seicho-
no-Ie practices, shinsokan ("practice of divine mind")
meditation. Cushions were brought out, and those who
wished took to the floor in a kneeling posture, holding the
hands clasped before the face, eyes closed. Others remained seated, but in reverent attention. The leader recited invocatory verses:

O God our Father, Who is the Original Soul, Who gives
    life to all living beings,
Fill my whole being with Your Infinite Spirit.
I live, move, and have my being not by my power

But by the Life of God that permeates the universe.
It is not my own power but the Omnipotent Power of God
That sustains all my actions
May the Holy Spirit Who has appeared to teach
    the Seicho-no-Ie Truth
Guide and protect me
In the Way.

When said in Japanese, this invocation is chanted in an ancient mode, but when said in English it is usually just spoken. It is followed by the leader's uttering a powerful, almost shrieked, cry: EE-EW! This strong vocal release marks, as it were, transition from one level of consciousness to another.

Then these words are said: "Having receded from the world of the five senses, I have now entered the world of Reality. Where I am now is the World of reality as it is." Then the following are said slowly three times each:

> The World of the Infinite Wisdom,
> The World of the Infinite Love,
> The World of the Infinite Life,
> The World of the Infinite Abundance,
> The World of the Infinite Joy,
> The World of the Infinite Harmony.

Then the meditation sinks into silence, but the meditator is expected to keep his mind from lethargy by visualizing as illumination and power the divine virtues flowing into him and filling him, until finally at the end he affirms: "O God our Father, Who is in Heaven in all brilliance, Your life of Grand Harmony is illuminating throughout the universe, and the universe is perfectly at peace now and forevermore." The hands are then clapped twice, and the eyes are opened.[28]

The evening ended with everyone making farewell chatter, and then departing into the night.

II

Who is Masaharu Taniguchi and what are his teachings?

He was born in 1893 in a village near Kobe, Japan; the site of his house is now covered by a reservoir. As a child, the future founder of Seicho-no-Ie seems to have been sensitive, emotional, and sometimes fearful. He felt things deeply and reflected much on them. He tells that as a small child he used to catch and kill frogs, thoughtless of the needless suffering he was inflicting on the amphibians. But when he later broke out in warts, his aunt (who raised him after the age of four) said it was because he had killed too many frogs. This affected him acutely, leading him to think about the invisible power of thought waves and moral cause and effect. He wondered if the pain of the dying frogs was returning upon him.[29] One has a picture of a pale, sensitive child, the type who is poor in sports but who, in his loneliness, has strange deep thoughts and intense feelings.

Like many such boys, he found his true world, the world of exciting intellectual and emotional life, only when he went to the university. At nineteen, he entered Waseda University in Tokyo. There he studied English literature, and became intoxicated with the ideas of men like Poe, Wilde, Baudelaire, and Schopenhauer. He went through a young romantic's infatuation with literary pessimism and sensibility; he liked Schopenhauer's idea that suffering is the core of life and pleasure only inconstant, and the thesis of Oscar Wilde that beauty is a value that transcends good and evil. Yet he later said that it was Wilde's absolutizing of beauty which led him to the thought of absolute perfection.

He spent only a year at Waseda, for along with all his intellectual passions the young knight of romantic sensibility also found time for a fervent romance with the daughter of a dock worker. His aunt disapproved of this relationship and cut off his allowance, forcing him to leave school, return to Kobe, and take a job.

Taniguchi took not one job but two, working during the day with a cotton company and at night as a translator. This, together with two more difficult affairs of the heart, led him to a state of extreme anxiety. He sought solace in the Omoto faith, and there found a helpful spiritual world view. He was attracted to Omoto's idea of a spiritual world, and to the promise it held out of social reform based on spiritual principles. He was one of five scribes who recorded Onisaburo Deguchi's *Spirit World Stories*. He took a job with Omoto as an editor of publications, and soon married a girl who was an Omoto employee.[30]

Taniguchi continued his avid reading, virtually devouring libraries of Eastern and Western philosophy, Buddhism, psychotherapy, and spirituality. In 1921 he left Omoto and moved back to Tokyo. This was when Omoto was beginning to suffer problems with the government, but in any case a man like Taniguchi would sooner or later have to strike out on his own spiritual path.

It was a period of economic uncertainty in Japan, and Taniguchi found no material advantage in the move to Tokyo. He and his wife lived in genteel poverty. But there were many others in the same situation in those days. Tokyo was at least Japan's intellectual hub, and was swarming with young men like himself, educated in Western as well as Eastern thought, threadbare but teeming with philosophical and literary talk, searching for directions. They haunted bookstalls and gathered in groups for conversations.

Taniguchi wrote an essay that attracted some attention in that milieu. It grew out of his philosophical musing, now turned idealistic. In this short book, he averred with determined optimism that suffering and evil cannot be real.

After the great Tokyo earthquake of 1923, Taniguchi and his family moved back to Kobe. He continued writing, and edited a magazine on psychic phenomena, but was barely able to support his wife and infant daughter. It was not until five years later, in 1928, that he had a series of experiences that set the ultimate course of his life.

One day, returning from worship at the famous Ikuta shrine in Kobe, he stopped at a bookstall and saw a copy of a work by the American New Thought writer Fenwicke Holmes called *The Law of Mind in Action*. Fenwicke Holmes was the brother of Ernest Holmes, founder of the Church of Religious Science, and both were distinguished New Thought teachers. New Thought is a primarily American spiritual movement that derives indirectly from the New England transcendentalism of men like Alcott and Emerson. Their principle that mind is the ground of the universe was developed by Phineas P. Quimby, Warren Felt Evans, and others, in the direction of healing, mental health, and prosperity through the power of mental affirmation. The basic thesis of New Thought is that thoughts are causative of a person's happiness and life situation. The Fenwicke Holmes book presents practical and detailed instructions on how this principle can be applied. Thus, a person, by affirming that he is healthy, prosperous, and joyful, can sow thought seeds around which these realities can take shape, and he will become healthy, prosperous, and joyful. This is the "universal law."

Shortly after reading the book, Taniguchi endeavored to put its teaching into practice in connection with obtaining a well-paying job as translator for an oil company. While waiting for a reply to his application, he prayed every day for half an hour about the position, all the while believing he had the job, affirming the reality of what he desired. When he was successful, he felt himself confirmed in a faith which much of his thinking had already anticipated.

Even as Taniguchi's financial situation improved, as if to test his convictions his daughter became seriously ill. That was especially disturbing since he considered that one's own thoughts create the circumstances of one's environment, and so he himself might well be responsible for the sickness. As he contemplated deeply upon this problem, reflections came to his mind along the lines of the old Buddhist scripture he had once read, but newly worded after his East-West education: "Matter is nothing; all things evolve from nothingness and take form according to thought patterns. . . . Your soul will be emancipated from all restrictions and obtain freedom if you do not adhere to matter by believing it to be real. See it for what it is! Infinite Supply will come. . . . You can draw out infinitude from 'nothingness' and have plenty left over. . . . Mind also does not exist! Only Reality exists! . . . Realize this truth! Immortal life will be restored here and now! Now! The eternal now! Resurrection is now! Live the Now!" This *Now* was the eternal Buddha and the eternal Christ.[31]

The meditation ended with a "light like a brilliant sunrise." One is reminded of the experience of brilliant light that Richard Bucke, in his *Cosmic Consciousness*, says often comes upon persons of unusual spiritual gifts in their early thirties. After this meditation, Taniguchi prayed in this spirit for his daughter's recovery, with full success.

The Seicho-no-Ie ("House of Growth") movement began shortly afterward, in 1930, with Taniguchi's inauguration of a periodical of that title to share his insights. It was first headquartered in Kobe, but he moved it to Tokyo in 1934. Demand for the magazine grew, including requests for back issues. In time, articles from the magazine were collected in a book called *Seimei no Jisso* ("Reality of Life"). These compiled writings now comprise some forty volumes.

Before long, producing the Seicho-no-Ie material was Taniguchi's vocation, and it quickly became a massive undertaking. In 1931, the fundamental scripture of Seicho-no-Ie, the *Holy Sutra, Nectarean Shower of Holy Doctrine*, now recited regularly by the faithful, was delivered to Taniguchi by an angel while he was in meditation.

Seicho-no-Ie went through changes of name, but it essentially has always been what it is today, not an ecclesiastical body in the strict sense, but a teaching organization created around the personality of Masaharu Taniguchi. It has an impressive headquarters building in Tokyo. It publishes books and periodicals, sponsors lectures, holds training sessions and seminars. Yet the fact that it has a charismatic leader, a distinctive teaching, particular spiritual practices such as shinsokan, and a body of committed followers makes it clearly a religious movement. In Japan, where there is much overlap of religious allegiance between almost all groups (except Christianity and Nichiren Shoshu), the interdenominational character of Seicho-no-Ie as a literary, inspirational movement (a "Truth Movement," advocates like to say) is clearer than in the United States. Here the character of society has led the movement to organize as a denomination. But here too it has many readers of the literature outside the church.

The growth and popularity of Seicho-no-Ie in Japan was evident from 1930 on. Thousands and then millions of Japanese found help in Taniguchi's teaching of the power of affirmation that reality is absolutely perfect, and that thought can change the pattern and mood of a life. Countless numbers thereby received strength to face triumphantly sickness, poverty, and reverses.

However, in the late 1930's and early 1940's emerged one of the most controversial aspects of Taniguchi's career: his apparent support of the extreme Japanese nationalism rampant in those days. Taniguchi taught that the Emperor was Ultimate Being, and wrote affirmative inspirational lines for soldiers in the Imperial Army. As a consequence, during the Occupation under General MacArthur he was on the list of those "purged" and forbidden to take part in public life. Even since the war, Taniguchi has been identified with causes commonly regarded in Japan as right-wing: support of display of the Japanese flag; demands for restoration of the prewar holiday commemorating the establishment of the Empire; organization of groups for teachers, students, and youth to compete with the frequently leftist alternatives.

However, Taniguchi and Seicho-no-Ie people argue that the thrust of his teachings is toward personal and world peace, and that to interpret Taniguchi's attitude toward Japan and its symbols as political or militaristic is a misconstruction. There is a sense in which this defense can probably be accepted. Taniguchi's affirmation of Japanese patriotic language and emblems must be seen in the light of the basic New Thought belief in the efficacy of word and symbol to hold up an ideal and thereby help it to coalesce as a manifestation of the perfect universal reality that underlies it. The large Japanese flag that hangs behind Taniguchi as he lectures may not necessarily imply chauvinism, as unfortunate as may be the memories it recalls, but rather may be a symbolic affirmation of the truth which that nation, like all nations, has to give the world. By New Thought principles, affirming the goodness of a nation and its heritage will work to bring into being the best that is potential in it. If you want a country to be good, say nothing bad about it, they would argue; New Thought has an almost taboo-like aversion to saying anything negative, or less than enthusiastically "affirming perfection," about anyone or anything. In Seicho-no-Ie, one prays for others by speaking of their perfection with faith in the causative power of thought and word. At least in the context of postwar Japan, whose spiritual malaise is partly bound up with a one-sided repression of salutary pride in culture and tradition, one can see the therapeutic possibilities of such patriotism. In any case, Seicho-no-Ie in America seems to have no particular political or nationalistic overtones.

III

The basic teachings of Seicho-no-Ie, which also imply a program, are outlined over and over. These are the basic points:[32]

1. Man is a child of God. This is taken to mean that he has God's perfect, divine quality within him.

2. The power of Word is applied as a means of manifesting this indwelling infinite quality. By "Word" is meant

prayer and especially the recitation of the *Holy Sutra*. This means that, as in most Eastern religions, words by their very sound or vibrations have an ability to express or isolate hitherto hidden qualities. Saying only good, positive things is a way of making visible the essential and eternal perfection of all things.

3. The phenomenal world that one sees and experiences reflects his thoughts. If you want to be happy, says Seicho-no-Ie, change your mind. One's environment will mirror his mind, bright or drab, hopeful or depressing. It is only a person's dark thoughts that cloud (for him) the real nature of the universe, which is perfect.

4. In Absolute Truth, all religions are one and the same. They all reflect the same spiritual ground, though they may take different form in different times and places.

5. Seicho-no-Ie teaches deliverance from feelings of guilt, holding that so long as man has a sense of sin, he can never realize that he is a perfect child of God and saved already.

6. The principle of reconciliation and perfect harmony is very important. To have the inner peace which comes from knowing that one is a child of God and perfect, it is essential to be reconciled with all things, that is, to accept all things gratefully as wholly good. This is the reason for the continual repetition of "Thank you very much" among Seicho-no-Ie people. The words express both an acceptance of other people and a total attitude of gratefulness to God.

These teachings are all reflected over and over in the writings of Taniguchi. For example:

> The flesh eye may see a snake swallowing a frog, but it is not the real aspect of life. A depraved appearance is not the real aspect of man. The form changes according to the

mind, however everything is good in the World of Reality. *Seicho-no-Ie's Philosophy* or principle of education that when one visualizes the Reality in his mind, its perfect aspect will be reflected in the manifest world and the manifest world will turn into an earthly heaven, has been proved by actual facts.[33]

7. The final principle is the meditation method, shin-sokan.

These principles are augmented by a set of seven statements, more program-oriented, called the Declaration.[34]

1. We strive not to be prejudiced against any sect or religion, but believe in the spiritual nature of man and live according to the spiritual truth of life.

2. We believe that to manifest fully the Great Life Principle leads to infinite power and plenty, and that the personality of every individual is immortal.

3. We study the Law of the Creative Spirit and make it known to all, so that humanity may follow the right way to infinite growth.

4. We believe that Love is the best nourishment for Life and that prayer, words of love, and praise are the creative Way of the Word, necessary to manifest Love.

5. We believe that we, Sons of God, have infinite power and plenty within ourselves and can attain absolute freedom by following the Creative Way of the Word.

6. We publish the monthly *Seicho-no-Ie* and other literature filled with good messages, so that all men may follow the creative Way of the good words and lead happy lives.

7. We organize movements to conquer suffering by following the right view of life, right living, and right education, and at last to bring the Kingdom of Heaven to earth.

The syncretistic nature of these teachings should be evident; while using terminology reminiscent of Christian and especially New Thought discourse, Taniguchi also alludes to the Buddha, his enlightenment and teaching of the nonreality of phenomenal existence, and to the Universal Buddha-Nature. At least one of Taniguchi's prayers addresses the Shinto goddess Amaterasu, regarded also as the universal divine reality. This terminological equation undergirds Taniguchi's assertion that "All religions come from one universal God."

The many books of Masaharu Taniguchi are filled with anecdotes that illustrate the application in daily life of these teachings, especially in overcoming emotional problems and in the healing of sickness. For example, he tells the story related to him of a woman who had been an attender at a short series of his lectures. This woman had suffered from a fibroid tumor of the uterus. When bathing with an intimate woman friend at a temple, she discussed it with her, and told the friend that her wedding night had been very unpleasant to her and that she had been unable to overcome a feeling that her husband was bestial and sex was filthy. The friend reminded her that Masaharu Taniguchi had explained that the union of male and female is the origin of creation and as clean as heaven and earth, and that "the life of Seicho-no-Ie is to accept anything meekly, the mind of rejection was wrong, it was necessary to be self-effaced and accept her husband meekly." The woman took this reminder to heart, and by the following day the tumor had practically disappeared. This is an obvious and typical example of the power of negative thought to produce illness, and of correct, positive understanding to remove it.[35]

A similar case is more complex, and shows ways in

which Taniguchi parallels psychoanalytic insights into hidden motivation. The motif of parents being responsible through their attitudes for the sickness of children is a recurring topic with Taniguchi, and is apparent here. A young girl introduced to Taniguchi seemed about seven months pregnant. But she was still a virgin and could not be pregnant. The inflammation was due to a fibroid tumor of the uterus. Surgery had been recommended, but it would have made her unable to bear children.

Obviously this case could not be one of conjugal inharmony, as the previous one was. Taniguchi tried to trace the case back. He found that the girl's mother had fits of asthma caused by the sight of cats. He found too that the asthma was probably no normal allergy, because it had started only when the mother had seen her husband's favorite mistress, who constantly was stroking a cat on her lap. The mother felt bitterness toward the mistress and the husband, and the daughter with the tumor picked up the dark, miserable feelings she effused. Taniguchi reports that after the two took a Seicho-no-Ie short course and overcame these passions, the asthma and the tumor both disappeared.[36]

The same technique is reported to work in educational problems as well. Taniguchi relates the case of a grade-school girl who did very poorly, finally receiving an F in arithmetic. But when she was taken to Seicho-no-Ie, she was told: "You are the daughter of God. It cannot be that you make poor grades in school." She believed this, and returning to school showed marked improvement, and successfully took the entrance examinations to high school. She also needed, or seemed to need, glasses as a correction for nearsightedness at one point. But she received from Seicho-no-Ie a firm belief that, "Man is originally perfect, so that there can be no nearsightedness," and soon had no problem with myopia.[37]

In his basic books, such as *The Truth of Life*, Taniguchi establishes the philosophical basis of these psychotherapeutic cures. Taniguchi's ideas remind one of humanistic psychologists such as Abraham Maslow, who taught that psychology should start by considering the "being state" when one feels totally, harmoniously, and all-sufficiently just alive, to be the "normal" point of reference rather than sickness states. Taniguchi frequently refers to the methods of Mesmer, Freud, Adler, and other hypnotists and analysts, but considers them incomplete insofar as they do not take into account his ontologizing, or making into a reality principle, absolute harmony and perfection.

Skillfully he calls teachers such as Christ, the Buddha, Mary Baker Eddy, and Tenrikyo's Miki Nakayama to witness that the one thought which is really curative is the thought that all is perfect. Taniguchi recognizes, though, that the unconscious is more powerful than the conscious. Thus he is always seeking ways to bring this realization of perfection to the level of the *un*conscious. Meditation, suggestion, chantings, and indirect teaching through experience are all helpful. Once a patient really understands that he is united with God and is perfect, then he can heal himself, for the best answers, Taniguchi once said, come from one's own lips when one is united with God.

However, Seicho-no-Ie always insists that medical help should be sought also, saying that if you *feel* ill, you need a doctor. Taniguchi continually worked in cooperation with doctors who appreciated what he had to give. Seicho-no-Ie healing was said to be possible by telepathy as well as by direct work with the patient, through the sending out of *nempa*, or "thought waves." As Taniguchi may have learned from the frogs he killed very early in life, "thought waves" can be positive or negative. Taniguchi believed that a positive example was the curing of his own daughter at the time of his spiritual transformation, for at the moment she was cured he was meditating and praying on her behalf on a streetcar some distance away.

IV

What are the dimensions of this movement? Seicho-no-Ie reports some three million adherents throughout the world. Most are in Japan, but in 1974 there were some seven thousand in the United States, and seventy thousand in Brazil, with a scattering elsewhere.

About 98 percent of the U.S. membership is of Japanese descent. However, the fact that Seicho-no-Ie is largely a publication movement means that its influence cannot be measured just in terms of formal membership, and this is particularly true in the light of the close relationship it has had with New Thought. Since the war, Taniguchi and Fenwicke Holmes, who so influenced him much earlier, have written a book together called *The Science of Faith*.[38] It was published in both English and Japanese. On his trips to America, Taniguchi has spoken in Religious Science churches and elsewhere to overflow crowds, mostly Occidental. Many of these people, while not formally joining Seicho-no-Ie, have doubtless been deeply influenced by Taniguchi's teachings, have obtained and read some of his translated texts, and have been reinforced in the New Thought faith by this proclamation of it from overseas.

It is interesting to note, in fact, that most of the Occidentals who have entered Seicho-no-Ie do *not* have a New Thought church background. As in the case of the optometrist, who was brought to Seicho-no-Ie through a Japanese friend, Seicho-no-Ie has happened to be their introduction to the New Thought world, and so was the wing of it they entered. Most Occidental New Thought people, while helped by Taniguchi, prefer to work with a church in their own cultural tradition.

In the United States there is a Seicho-no-Ie church and center in Hawaii, and three churches on the mainland, in Gardena (a suburb of Los Angeles), San Jose, and Seattle. There are also about sixty-five home meetings.

Seicho-no-Ie first came to the United States in 1938 when Masaharu Matsuda, Tsuruta Yozan, and Mrs. Taneko Shimazu arrived here after completing training sessions in Japan. Mr. Matsuda went to Denver, where he engaged in interesting discussions with the Church of Divine Science, a New Thought denomination headquartered there, but the Seicho-no-Ie work took root on the West Coast among the Japanese-American population. In 1941 Unosuke Karatsu became the first lecturer in Los Angeles.

The training sessions are the heart of the Seicho-no-Ie movement. Fifteen training centers are located throughout Japan. Trainees live at the centers for ten to fifteen days to receive intensive study and experience to lead them to realize the truth of the indwelling Divine Nature. Many of the leaders of the movement in America, at least those able to understand Japanese, have attended these sessions. English-language sessions have been held regularly in Gardena since 1969, but thus far they have been only of three days' duration.

After the war, a Seicho-no-Ie church was established in Los Angeles. In 1966 the church and headquarters were moved to beautiful new buildings in Gardena. The training center building was completed adjacent to it in 1971. The church is governed by an elected board, but a minister is sent out from the headquarters in Japan to oversee the spiritual functions. The Gardena church has an "English Department" which supervises instruction in that language. In the United States there are twenty-four missionaries (unpaid) and five lecturers, designated after training by Taniguchi. A Hawaii-raised minister, the Reverend Paul Kikumoto, took charge of the work in 1973.

Apart from translation into English, the worship and teaching has not changed in crossing the ocean. It would appear this is the way the committed American members of both Japanese and Occidental descent want it. They are strongly attracted to the personality of Taniguchi and to the simplicity of the teachings. They speak of him with reverence and want to do things as he wants them done, and they feel that the teachings are very modern and scientific as they stand, in no need of revision.

What sort of person is attracted to Seicho-no-Ie? Whether Oriental or Occidental, Americans in the movement seem to be largely middle-class, outwardly comfortable, educated people who have nonetheless been inwardly seekers. Without probing for deeper psychological motivations, one is struck by the observation that what has been most persuasive about Seicho-no-Ie to them is its optimism—its ability to affirm that all is indeed good and perfect, that there is a solution within one to every problem, a cure to every ill, and a final truth available in this troubled world, a truth that can be utilized and experienced, not just learned.

The Seicho-no-Ie churches have the social activities typical of American churches: picnics, breakfasts, bazaars, New Year's celebrations. A party is held on Taniguchi's birthday. There is no formal initiation into membership; one "joins" by subscribing to the magazine *Seicho-no-Ie,*

or just by attending the church or any of the home meetings. However, members are expected to make a monthly
donation. Serious members will practice shinsokan meditation privately every day and recite daily readings from
the *Holy Sutra*. Reading the *Holy Sutra* is regarded as a
purification ceremony: it cleanses the inner self just as a
bath cleanses the outer. As it is read, thoughts of anger
and ill will are dissolved.

V

In the summer of 1972, I visited the Gardena church for
a Sunday morning service. It is a tasteful modern building
surrounded by exceptionally attractive Japanese landscaping. Entering, I saw at the front a simple altar under a
scroll bearing only the Japanese characters for the word
jisso ("reality"). Reality alone is the object of worship.
The altar bore flowers, and the hanging zigzag strips of
paper called *gohei*, which are the Shinto symbol of divine
presence. Beside the altar stood branch candelabra and,
on each side, American and Seicho-no-Ie flags. On various
walls were signs saying "*Arigato gozaimasu*" and the English equivalent, "Thank you very much." The congregation
was mostly Japanese, with a sprinkling of Caucasians.

The service opened with an exchange of the thanking
greeting between the leader and the congregation. That
was followed with reverencing the altar with bows and
claps in the clipped, almost military manner characteristic
of Japanese worship. Next came a hymn by Taniguchi.

After the hymn came shinsokan meditation, introduced
in the usual way with the affirmations chanted in Japanese
and repeated in a quiet voice in English, culminating in
the striking yell.

Following this brief service, the assembly broke into

English-language and Japanese-language groups for instruction. The English group went to the new training center to sit on folding chairs in a spotlessly clean hall. There was a table burdened with literature near the door. The group was comprised of five or six Caucasians and about a dozen Japanese-Americans.

The address, by a young Japanese-American lay missionary who spoke fluently and well, was on the topic of sickness. He started with reference to a newspaper article on psychophysiological origins of illness, which indicated that now even conventional doctors believe that a high percentage of illnesses can be traced to psychological origins. The speaker noted that Taniguchi was saying the same thing years before, and even more radically. He mentioned the three- or four-day training sessions in which one gets to realize that mind is cause. The purest way is to live so close to God in gratitude that one doesn't need to rely on medicines or doctors at all. He spoke of a Seicho-no-Ie practice of writing out on paper things that are in the way of this realization, and then burning the paper while the *Holy Sutra* is recited.

The key to therapy, he said, is repentance with tears. He spoke of an experience with paralysis in his own son. Up to the age of fourteen, he said, illness in children is 100 percent a reflection of the parents' mind. He had thought he was a good father to his boy, and had played baseball with him every evening. But the games had often ended in tears as he tried to push the son too hard to play well. Through a conference he had with Taniguchi, he realized that it was he who had to repent. He had been torturing the boy, forcing him to take refuge in the paralysis. He told similar stories of a woman with cancer who had been fighting with her daughter-in-law for five years, and of a woman with an allergy to sunshine who had been hating her mother for dying when she was one year old and thus "abandoning" her child.

VI

On a rainy day in August of 1972, I attended a Seicho-no-Ie training session, and visited discussion groups of teen-agers present. This experience gave me a new kind of insight into the movement: the concerns and questions of young people interested or involved in it one way or another, and the manner in which lay leaders responded.

The first group I visited was sitting in a circle in the church talking about the drug problem. The adult leader was raising questions about whether drugs should be legalized, and what sort of response parents should make to children who use drugs. The group, both leaders and teen-agers, was all Japanese-American. There was little response from the young people, but an older woman present as an assistant leader made some strong points. She emphasized that Seicho-no-Ie says to "look at the good side" of every situation. Parents should not reject children whose lives have been damaged by drug use, but should love the good that is still in them. The church should provide a positive alternative to bad company, and if it does so, it has to be "a fun place to go." Seicho-no-Ie has an opportunity here, since it is always positive, and is "a living, open kind of thing."

Someone else raised a question, directed in part to me, about Shinto ornaments such as the *gohei* and the ancestral tablets in the church. Several in the group seemed quite curious about the extent of Shinto heritage remaining. Seicho-no-Ie churches, like nearly all Japanese religions today, have a monthly service on behalf of the departed, who are commemorated by wooden tablets bearing their names. In this church, these are located in a parish hall. The practice is probably originally Chinese and Buddhist, but is now associated with Shinto shrines and New Religions as much as with the temple.

I next visited a group discussing psychic matters. It was led by an enthusiastic, capable young man who had completed a three-week training session in Japan, and was comprised of about a dozen teen-agers, including two or three Caucasians. This group was quite vocal and clearly very much interested in the topic. The Caucasians gave the impression of wanting deeply to believe in spirits, psychic phenomena, and Seicho-no-Ie philosophy, but being always held back by a painful skepticism. The leader presented the conventional Seicho-no-Ie answer to everything, in a manner that communicated modesty and openness. When asked about psychic happenings, ESP, and so forth, he acknowledged the reality of this phenomenon, but said that it develops with fasting and meditation. Some people may have it naturally, but it may be more than they can handle, like driving a semi truck with a practice license.

A Japanese-American girl spoke of having had something like out-of-the-body experiences. They were unwanted, and took the form of her seeming to move in bed just before going to sleep. She said that meditation had brought them on, and she implied that meditation was dangerous. The leader said that this might be the result of some kinds of meditation, but not shinsokan, which is not making the mind vacant but filling it with beautiful thoughts. But the girl said that shinsokan was among the kinds of meditation she had tried, and she thought it didn't work. The leader reemphasized that Taniguchi says one must meditate on the good; emptying the mind, as in Zen, can indeed be dangerous for those not prepared for it. One must not let the mind wander in meditation—one must be in the now, the Eternal Now, and pay attention all the time. A wandering mind is what destroys perfection. A Caucasian affirmed that living in the Eternal Now was what she valued so much.

The leader went on to say that through this kind of positive meditation the higher natures—the "etheric body"—take over the mind. He showed a diagram which indicated that, according to Taniguchi's teaching, only 5 percent of one's mind is his own present, private personality. The remainder is composed of memory, emotions, and regional, national, and racial constituents. Beneath all of this is superconsciousness—God. You are not God himself, he said, but part of God, as a child is of his mother. You do not individually have all the qualities of God, but the Infinite is within each of us.

A Caucasian girl objected that she couldn't believe she was God. The leader answered that we are each a radiation of the light source. Everything reflects the wisdom and power of God. Look at the perfection of the human body, for example.

The discussion then turned to reincarnation. It was said that Seicho-no-Ie believes in reincarnation, since God is infinitely just. Otherwise, much in life would be unfair. You are born when your vibrations in the spiritual world are in tune with those of an earthly time, place, and set of prospective parents. Here is an echo of Omoto and World Messianity belief in a prenatal spiritual world where spirits dwell between incarnations.

The leader said that a spirit has the prerogative of refusing to be born; everyone makes a choice to enter into this world and go through it. But going through the world is educative; it is for the benefit of the spirit. This also reflects the dictum that mind, spirit, is prior; it is for its benefit that experience in the world is undergone.

The Caucasian girl retorted that it doesn't seem as though this were so in everyday life. What of a child born into a situation with coarse, brutal parents and without the conscious spiritual knowledge to understand the situation? The leader said that this child will rebel against his parents, and cause the parents to undergo a punishment that will be ultimately beneficial to them, so it balances out. The girl replied that the parents will just say they don't care.

The leader started to reply: "Well, they may say that . . ." The other interjected, "Spirit is so weak, gentle, disappears . . ."

Shortly afterward everyone gathered in the church for instruction and practice in shinsokan. The instructor was the same young man who had led the last discussion.

He opened by saying: You don't like to pray. You would rather eat, play, read. You ask, How can meditation give me anything? It can give you lots of things, both material and spiritual. It can make your mind bright and happy, and then anything can come. It can give you health. If you can laugh off things that make you angry, it helps you. This is how meditation works. It is not a fairy tale. It means that negative things can't get to you. You can't bring darkness to an area of light. If you are a light thing through shinsokan, you can be better. You make friends, you have a better chance of being promoted.

The speaker said that as a boy he used to pray for things like a bicycle, and was disappointed when no bicycle came. But prayer does work—through the subconscious mind. If you pray, you will eventually get what you prayed for. It's just like planting a seed. The subconscious mind is one with God: God and man are one. Other people are God too. If you have negative thoughts toward them, you are not right with God. You have to be grateful.

Shinsokan meditation is the most important way to change your mind. Prayer is more powerful than knowledge. As you sit in shinsokan, think on the perfection of God . . . God is good, wonderful, beautiful. You have to bring *light* in. You have to realize that if someone insults you, it's because you deserve it. Smile back. He won't insult you next time. The insult is caused by dark thoughts in your mind.

He said to concentrate, with hands folded over the nose, and elbows hanging free. We began shinsokan. The opening words chanted in Japanese ending in a high shriek seemed to startle one into an altered state of consciousness. I found that holding the hands up produced an intolerable strain, although the position was said to be comfortable. I tried (as do many Occidentals) to continue the shinsokan meditation without that particular posture. I felt that somehow this was wrong, though, as I looked at the sea of people, mostly Japanese, meditating in identical posture, and realized that the collective, group technique, suggesting an army in conformity as it seeks the Perfect, is part of the Seicho-no-Ie mystique. A specific practice is another way of suggesting the submergence of the obstreperous ego with its great capacity for dark thoughts.

It is, however, the philosophy as much as the practice which brings Westerners to Seicho-no-Ie. Later I talked with a Caucasian couple who had been with the movement for about ten years. They were intelligent and well-educated. Both are teachers, and the wife is a graduate in psychology. They had long been spiritual seekers, but had not been in New Thought religious movements. They first heard about Seicho-no-Ie through a chiropractor, who was not a member of Seicho-no-Ie but well informed about unusual religious movements and a friend of Seicho-no-Ie. (It is interesting to note in passing that chiropractors, probably because of their marginal position in American professional life, are often led to involvement in new spiritual paths.)

This couple became active in the original Los Angeles Seicho-no-Ie group that met in an upper room, and expressed considerable feeling for those days of a small group with intense spiritual life. They talked of several people who overcame severe physical or emotional handicaps in those days. They recalled what great affection they, and others, showed for Taniguchi and his wife on their visits to America. They talked of the love of Japanese culture they had acquired through Seicho-no-Ie, though they have never been to Japan.

They said that what struck them about Seicho-no-Ie, in contrast to some Western psychological theories, is the fundamental teaching that people are perfect, and that this perfection can be brought out. That teaching is not new, but has been newly stated as the message of Seicho-no-Ie. It embodies a practical approach to life which says that one doesn't have to be pessimistic, but can be continually cheerful. They also liked the concept of the unity of all peoples and religions.

To summarize the teaching again: We are all children of God and not children of sin; this phenomenal world is a reflection of your own mind as it appears to you. If you wish to be happy and live in a happy world, have a happy mind. The power of the word is central because word is the Creator of the spiritual universe. All religions express this and so are basically one and the same. As a child of God, you are already immaculate and redeemed. Reconcile yourself with everyone and everything and manifest genuine peace and happiness. Shinsokan meditation manifests inner perfection, because of God's infinite wisdom, infinite love, infinite life, infinite abundance, infinite joy, and infinite harmony.

More than any other major Japanese New Religion, Seicho-no-Ie reflects the direct influence of Western thought. Yet in some of its deepest attitudes it is intensely Japanese even as it expresses itself in Western psychological and New Thought language. Taniguchi seems almost to embody something of the painful quest of modern Japan for an identity between East and West, and a way of resolving it which can have universal appeal.

READING SELECTION

The following passage from Taniguchi's basic book illustrates his attempt to reconcile East and West by assimilating Christ and Buddha, and also gives an insight into some fundamental Seicho-no-Ie teachings.

But, according to Buddhism the Great Life, Father, having sent to this world His only son Bodhisattva Hozo who, after going through numberless sufferings and ascetic practices in our place, became *Amida* (Eternal Buddha), and we now have only to leave everything to him for our salvation without much ascetic practice.

Thus, in both Christianity and Buddhism, Christ and Amida are two manifestations of the same Savior, Son of

God, sent by the Great Life, Father, for our perfect freedom from the sufferings of existence.

Considering the fact that the Great Life, Father, sent Christ and Amida as our Saviors, He is not at all pleased to see us suffer in life. In case growth is impossible without suffering on account of lack of enlightenment of Soul, God may have no other way than to give us pain and diseases, but with the tender heart of Father, He must want to make His son (Man) grow with as little suffering as possible.

"Seicho-no-Ie" has been born to enlighten the Soul of Man after the tender heart of the Great Love (Father) and the Great Saviors (Christ and Amida). And having been awakened to the fact that if Man only walks in "the right path of growth" never going astray, he can give his Soul the infinite growth making his life pleasant, without the necessary pain to reflect upon himself. We are studying "the right path of growth" (to tell the truth, when I take up my pen, Divine inspiration comes over me and, very often I can write down such truth as I had not even thought of) and convey it to you to enlighten your Souls that you may have as little pain and disease as possible, through which many souls would have undergone certain psycho-chemical agitations of cathartic process.

—Masaharu Taniguchi, Ph.D., *The Truth of Life* (Tokyo: Seicho-no-Ie Foundation, 1961), pp. 25–27.

6

Perfect Liberty

I

Among the most enchanting of the Japanese New Religions is one called simply Perfect Liberty. Its adherents tend to have a gaiety and charm that is irresistible, and its teachings project boundless optimism about man and his potentials. PL, as it is often called, believes that man is meant to enjoy life and that play is of great spiritual value.

There is, however, far more to this faith than games. For one thing, Perfect Liberty is fascinating because its history images clearly the transitions through which Japanese religion has passed in its process of adapting to the modern world. In the three successive religious leaders who have dominated the tradition that is now Perfect Liberty, we see a movement from the ancient Japanese religion of sacred mountains, holy trees, and Zen meditation to the modern businessman's Japan of golf and Rotary clubs.

Yet the tradition has long had an interaction with the business world, just as for centuries Japan has been a nation of shopkeepers. The first man in the series, Tokumitsu Kanada (1863–1919), was a fairly well-to-do Osaka cutlery dealer who was also very much attracted to the esoteric Buddhist Shingon tradition and a mountain faith, Mitake-kyo. Both of these heritages have very deep roots in Japan. Shingon, brought from China early in the ninth century and for several centuries thereafter the dominant expression of Buddhism in Japan, has had an incomparable effect on Japanese culture. Its chief monastery, on Mt. Koya (which Kanada is said to have visited over a hundred times), is a treasure-house of both art and spiritual practices.[39]

Shingon's central conviction is that everything and every person is an expression of Dainichi, the "Great Sun Buddha," which really means the Buddha-essence of the universe or being itself as it is perceived by an enlightened mind. Through practices involving hand gestures (mudras), chanting (mantras), and meditation, one can identify himself with the cosmos in its marvelous essence and allow it to shine forth through him and all he does, and so become a Buddha in this body, in this lifetime. Art and ritual are extremely important to Shingon, since they are ways of *demonstrating* the splendor of the Buddha-nature locked in all persons and all things. In the same spirit, acting out ritual and artistic creativity are ways of training the mind to that sensitivity and concentration which makes one a Buddha, even as what he makes allows the imprisoned glory to radiate out of the lumpish raw materials of stone, wood, metal, and pigment.

Mitake-kyo, the other ancient faith in which Tokumitsu Kanada was interested, is one of several Shinto-related religions which make the climbing of sacred mountains a religious exercise. Mountain religion in Japan goes back to the misty days of prehistoric myth and magic. Ancient shamans would practice great austerities in the mountains to obtain wizard powers, and gods were believed to descend upon mountaintops. After the introduction of Buddhism and especially Shingon, a close alliance between Shingon and the even older mountain faith grew up. It was expressed in the orders of mountain priests called *yamabushi*. These gay, fierce adepts, until recently a major element in Japanese religion, and still found in some places, would go into the mountains, undergo potent initiations—leaping over fires, standing under waterfalls, walking on hot coals, being suspended by the heels over sheer cliffs, meditating in solitude all winter—and upon return to their villages would practice spiritualism and healing.

As both a merchant and a leader of this sort of faith, Kanada lived a varied life. He would go on mountain pilgrimages, do faith healing, and give financial advice. He developed a healing practice called *ofurigae* by which he would take onto himself the illnesses of his followers. (Interestingly, the name is just a word for a financial transaction, *furigae*, plus the honorific *o*.) Following the example of the founder of Shingon, Kobo Daishi, Kanada once leaped from a cliff and knocked himself unconscious, claiming thereby to receive spiritual illumination.[40]

In 1912, Tokumitsu Kanada founded a sect within Mitake-kyo called Shinto-Tokumitsu-kyo (meaning, roughly, "The Divine Way as taught by Tokumitsu"). The same year a learned Zen priest, Tokuharu Miki, joined him. Miki had been the incumbent of seven Zen temples successively over the preceding thirty years, but being unable to support his family through his priesthood alone, he had also tried various business ventures, all of which failed. Discouraged with Zen's inability to answer his spiritual problems, and in despondency over his many reverses, Miki eagerly received the teaching that Kanada offered.

He learned of its basis in Shingon esoteric pantheism, its use of an eclectic selection of meditation and ascetic practices to develop hidden inner powers of mind and soul, its provision of practical results in health and prosperity. Soon Miki had become a teacher of the new faith and Kanada's closest associate. By 1916, Miki's oldest son—the same man who today is *oshieoya*, or patriarch, of the worldwide Perfect Liberty movement—was in training for the priesthood of the Shinto-Tokumitsu-kyo faith.

At his death in 1919, Kanada predicted that a "sincere and faithful man" would come and add three principles to the eighteen he had already formulated. He also commanded Miki to plant a *himorogi* (an ancient name for a sacred tree in Shinto) and worship before it daily.

Miki did so. He meditated at the small tree every day, in cold and heat, rain, snow, or fair weather, for five years. At the end of this time, he realized that he himself was the coming one whom Kanada had promised. He broke with the dwindling Shinto-Tokumitsu-kyo and formed a new religion of his own, Jindo-Tokumitsu-kyo ("The Human Way as taught by Tokumitsu"). It was registered as a part of Fuso-kyo, another Shinto mountain sect. Miki's faith stressed somewhat less the esoteric aspects of the other Tokumitsu teaching. It emphasized instead the importance of right family and social relationships.[41]

In 1931 the name was changed to Hito no Michi ("Way of Man"). In those days the new religion flourished and claimed a million members. But like many other groups it fell afoul of the militaristic government. In 1936, when the movement was about to undergo investigation, the aging Tokuharu Miki passed the leadership to his son, Tokuchika Miki (1900–), the present *oshieoya*. Persecution ensued for alleged failure of the religion to support the imperial system. After Tokuharu died in 1939, Hito no Michi was ordered to disband. Finally, in May 1945 Tokuchika was imprisoned and was not released until October of that year, after the war had ended.

In the postwar years Miki successfully revived the faith to which he had fallen heir, and shaped it to his own mold. In 1946 he founded a temple on the island of Kyushu, and renamed the group PL Kyodan ("PL Religious Association"). The letters "PL" stood for the English words "Perfect Liberty," and the group attracted immediate attention as the first and only native Japanese religion to have English words in its title. In those early days of the Occupation, American words, attitudes, and imports had great prestige, while what was distinctly Japanese seemed second-rate. PL, like other new religions, tried to adopt modern, cosmopolitan attitudes and symbols. Miki said that English was the chief international language, and that by using an English title his faith affirmed that it had a message for all mankind. He rewrote the principles of Hito no Michi, starting off his list with his great central concept, "Life is Art."

PL prospered in the postwar years. After several changes, in 1953 the headquarters was located on twenty-five hundred acres of land near Osaka. The site now supports a flourishing spiritual community. There is a great temple, a peace tower designed by Miki, and a model town of three thousand population. A hospital emphasizes experimental work in psychosomatic medicine: an elaborate data computer system files extensive psychological and life-history information about each patient and attempts to relate it to the pathological symptoms. A characteristic New Religions emphasis on popular education is present —there is a language institute, and there are schools from kindergarten through junior college, together with student residences and instruction halls. Finally, the headquarters site boasts a thirty-six-hole golf course, featuring attractive young girl "caddiettes." All of this is set amid thousands of gorgeous cherry trees.

The central personality at the headquarters is, of course, the *oshieoya* ("teaching parent," i.e., patriarch), Tokuchika Miki himself. He presides over this headquarters miniature paradise and over the faith. He is clearly the charismatic center of this world. With his graying temples, his distinguished profile, his confident smile, his glasses rimmed with dark plastic, he looks the part of a modern corporation executive. This impression is only reinforced when he wears a Western suit with conservative tie. But on ceremonial occasions he exchanges Madison Avenue apparel for a shimmering blue-and-gold cope and a high, two-peaked miter suggesting—despite the executive glasses—the pomp of fairyland ritual.

But in either role, the *oshieoya* is believed to have a mysterious and unique divine power. He can give *mioshie*, divine instruction, not only generally but also individually to persons who request it for their particular problems. His blessings and healings have unusual potency. When he appears in audiences or in the context of rituals in the great temples, all eyes are upon him. In every PL service around the world, the *oshieoya* is thanked for the benefits he has brought mankind, alike in his teachings and his mediation of divine power to man. Yet, together with all this, he plays golf and wears tailored suits in a world far different from that of his boyhood apprenticeship in a mountain sect. He is, one might say, an ancient shaman operating out of a twentieth-century board room.

In January 1960, Tokuhito Miki, nephew of the present

oshieoya, was named his future successor. A vigorous and personable young man, he is an officer in the Osaka Rotary Club.

In his work of spiritual guidance of the two and a half million members worldwide of PL (five thousand of whom are in the United States, half being Oriental and half Caucasian or black), the *oshieoya* is assisted by a panel of men called *oya* ("parents"). They have been trained and ordained by the *oshieoya* for the work of spiritual discernment, instruction, and healing. One of them, Jiro Yano, is now resident in the United States.

II

What is it that the *oshieoya* teaches? Perfect Liberty summarizes its beliefs about God, man, and life in what are called the Twenty-one Precepts, composed by Tokuchika Miki as a modification of the old Hito no Michi doctrine shortly after the war. They are as follows:

1. Life is Art.
2. Man's life is a succession of "self-expressions."
3. Man is a manifestation of God.
4. Man suffers if he fails to express himself.
5. Man loses his true self when swayed by feelings or emotions.
6. Man's true self is revealed when his ego is effaced.
7. All things exist in mutual relationship to one another.
8. Live radiantly as the sun.
9. All men are equal.
10. Strive for creating mutual happiness.
11. Have true faith in God.

12. There is a way (function) peculiar to every "name" (existence).

13. There is a way for men, and there is another for women.

14. All is for world peace.

15. All is a mirror.

16. All things progress and develop.

17. Comprehend what is most essential.

18. At every moment man stands at the crossroads of good and evil.

19. Act when your intuition dictates.

20. Live in perfect unity of mind and matter.

21. Live in Perfect Liberty.

This interesting list is in part a crossroads of East Asian philosophies. Numbers 5 to 8 are clearly Buddhist; numbers 12, 13, 17, and 19 suggest the Taoist-tinctured Neo-Confucian philosophy. But for Perfect Liberty the key concept is the first, "Life is Art," and in it lies the faith's distinctive contribution to religious life.

Perhaps the roots of "Life is Art" lie in Shingon's high concept of the role of art in spiritual realization. Through it, this expansive form of Buddhism said, we overcome the blinders imposed by narrow egoistic goals and emotion-beclouded vision. We can then act like a Buddha, freely surveying, reflecting, and creating the world, and become what we act out in self-expression.

Harry Thomsen has also suggested that in the "Life is Art" concept the two Mikis were influenced by Omoto, for Onisaburo Deguchi also made much of the concept of art.[42] He said that God is the first artist, and that the art of man is based on God's divine model of creativity. He proclaimed also that art is for all people, not for just the talented few, as a means of expressing personality and adding joy to daily tasks. Deguchi taught his followers all to have a form of artistic expression.

For Tokuchika Miki, however, the emphasis is on seeing the total pattern of one's life—vocation, marriage, interests, habits—as a single, unified piece of work constructed as an artist paints a picture. It is a matter of what we now call life-style. Art that is created to be viewed or heard is only a metaphor for seeing the whole of one's life as a work of art.

Miki emphasizes, in his book *Jinsei wa Geijutsu dearu* ("Human Life is Art"),[43] that life means a struggle to overcome limitations. It is impossible, of course, for man to overcome all finitude in the absolute sense. This inability to do what life seems to want to do gives rise to all sorts of conflicts, compensations, and finally despair. Man's striving for health, money, success, or pleasure may produce results for a while, but sooner or later it runs up against the outer limits of what is possible in a single finite lifetime. One realizes then that it is necessary to base happiness on something other than these things, or else see life only as defeat.

Art is also a striving to overcome limitation, but it works in a different way from striving for gain or pleasure. It is molding what is outside of one into a form that is both true to its own nature and an expression of the artist. The sculptor respects the grain of his wood or stone, yet he also makes his work show something of his soul. It should produce in viewers the response, "This is the way so-and-so respected the grain of wood or stone, and showed us what *it* was trying to say, and in so doing told us something about himself too."

Yet in a deeper sense the artist does infinitize himself,

for by blending with the nature of his material, which in turn is continuous with the infinite cosmos, he breaks down barriers around himself. He makes the very limits themselves tools and material, and shapes them into ornamented apertures.

So it is that a life itself can be a work of art by a master artist, and everyone can be a master artist in this medium. He can show what the material itself—as an expression of God—is trying to say, and he can infinitize himself through it. Art is a way to infinitize oneself, but it does so precisely by accepting, manipulating, and using limits. A painting is great because it limits the patches of the various colors, and makes them balance and contrast with one another in exactly the right way. A piece of sculpture is great because it sets just the right limits to a piece of wood or stone. A cathedral is great because of the way it limits space. Art does not rail against finitude, but taking it for granted, arranges it in a way that respects it, brings out its nature, and makes of it a bridge to the larger units of which each finite particular is a part, and so on to the unbounded.

The Twenty-one Precepts of PL provide a set of guidelines for this arrangement of the parts of life into a series of self-expressions that cumulatively become a masterpiece of art. They indicate that this requires freely expressing one's individuality in a particular vocation and life-style. They also point out the paradoxical truth that one's true individuality cannot be expressed to the highest degree unless one is completely free of egoistic desire and selfish attitudes. Like an artist simply bringing out the innate potentiality of his medium, one must be in a state of objectivity, dedicated to the welfare of all mankind, as he brings out the potentiality of the medium—even though the medium be his own life. This is summed up in the important concept of *misasage,* sincere dedication. Working for others in this spirit of unselfish giving is the way one brings out his genuine personality—it is finding oneself by losing oneself. It is paradoxical but true, PL rightly insists, that the true individuality of a life-artist is expressed only when he loses himself in his creation, or, better, in service and cooperation with others.

Each piece of art is different; this is a characteristic of artistic creations as over against mass-produced products. The life-artist works with, rather than against, the limits imposed by whether one is male or female, by his ingrained personality style, and by his situation in space and time. He must intuit the meaning of the particular place, time, and role in which he is situated. He then must accept that the tools and media of this work of art are mind and matter, and that they must go together, as the Precepts tell us. This means using the limits—the person and the situation—to make something special, unique, never seen before or since, for the power of everything finite, artistically, is that it is different.

III

The attitude of mind required to see and implement the artistic possibilities of the moment, and of all life, is called *makoto,* usually translated "sincerity." *Makoto,* a common word in Japanese philosophy, means a bright, pure, fresh heart and soul, undivided in its purpose and openness, and therefore capable of intuiting the wholeness of a situation. It is unblemished by emotion or ulterior motives.

The person who has *makoto,* whose life has become a work of art moment by moment, who wonderfully blends with his situation in life, as a well-placed statue or painting with its environment, has triumphed over limitation. Therefore he is living in "Perfect Liberty." That is the goal of the faith, and so is selected as its name.

A little booklet called *Self Lib* put out by the church states it this way: "Illness and accidents occur from 'shorting out' the power from Great Nature. . . . Do one thing at a time and do it as skillfully and as artistically as you know how. . . . One of life's great arts is how we express ourselves in our daily work. . . . Think of art as meaning every breath you take, every thought that crosses your mind, everything you do. The total *you* is art. . . . Are you good, bad, or indifferent?"

In Perfect Liberty, one is not left to his own devices— any more than is a novice in an art school—as he constructs his life into a work of art. The church provides mentors who are constructive art critics, or (to shift to the analogy of sports, which is also favored by PL) coaches. Instruction is given in sermons in a general way. But individual guidance from God and man is also imparted in the processes called *mishirase* and *mioshie*. These may be rendered "divine warning" and "divine instruction."

The presupposition which makes the artistic life possible (as a joyous rather than a tragic thing) is that man is an expression of God. We are part of God's great canvas, and it is meant to be right. Meaning and beauty and purpose lie behind it; even our limitations and frustrations play the role in God's work that patches of light and dark do on the painter's board. Therefore we can assume that ill things which happen to us are messages God is sending to provoke us to change something in our lives to make them more perfect as works of art, and so more satisfactory fragments of God's work.

Disease, reverses, and unhappiness are interpreted by

Perfect Liberty in this way. They are *mishirase,* divine warnings. In each there is a message that something is wrong and should be changed. Ours is not a chaotic universe in which pointless misfortune happens, Perfect Liberty insists. Bad things are always caused by mistakes and tell us of a situation it is within our power to correct, or at least to make into an artistic expression—one can even die, or suffer injustice, beautifully.

If an individual has a question concerning the interpretation of a *mishirase,* or regarding his spiritual life, he has a divinely guided counselor in the *oshieoya* or one of the *oya.* The procedure for receiving *mioshie,* or divine instruction, from one of these "coaches" is to write the question out on a prepared form and give it to one's minister, who forwards it. The minister receives the answer back in a week or two. He then takes it to the petitioner's home, and after prayer, gives it to him in a solemn and reverent manner. The *mioshie* might be something like this: that the individual is at a turning point in his life and must change, that he must have a different attitude toward his family, that he is sick because of a grudge he holds, that he must pray more, and the like. To be meaningful, the *mioshie* must be put into practice with *makoto.*

The principal form of prayer in Perfect Liberty is the *oyashikiri,* a distinctive form to which great effectiveness is ascribed. Emphasis is placed on the gestures used in this prayer; such emphasis is a part of the general stress on ritual in PL, which is really a natural consequence of the "Life is Art" motif. However, in situations where the hand gestures would be inappropriate it may be said only inwardly.

The *oyashikiri* is properly said before the PL talisman,

a consecrated paper displaying a tiny sun with twenty-one rays. The individual stands erect, bows, folds the hands over the waist, places them palms together over the lips, then raises them over the forehead to make a large circle like a sun. While doing this he chants slowly "Mi-oya-Okami Oyashikiri" (literally, something like "O Parent God, reconciliation with the Parent"). Basically, the *oyashikiri* is thought to be a way of identification with God, and so with the source of power. A PL tract says this about the *oyashikiri:*

> Millions of PL people are being saved by Oyashikiri Prayer. OYASHIKIRI PRAYER is uniquely PL. It is based on PL's 21 Precepts. PL Precepts say, "Life is Art. Man's life is a succession of self-expressions." Your prayers are expressions of your inner-self. In prayers you may listen to God, you may thank God, you may petition God. In doing so, you become merged with God through OYASHIKIRI prayer. Your whole being is completely united with the Great Nature. You realize yourself being integrated with the Universe. Your inner soul shines to the fullest extent. Your resolution and volition receive God's blessing. Miracles come to you through OYASHIKIRI as certain as night follows day.[44]

This passage casts some light on the PL concept of God. PL people say that while different people think of God on their own level of recognition, God is ultimately not to be conceived as personal. God is the one universal, the Universe itself. The Neo-Confucian term "Great Nature" is often used—Nature, but Nature in a transcendent sense that includes the Ground of mind and consciousness as well as of natural law.

IV

The graceful ritual of PL worship expresses the validity of artistic expression as a spiritual way. But the PL service also includes instruction and testimonials that show the importance of the individual and his spiritual development.

In the summer of 1972 I attended a PL service in a small church in the United States. About twenty-five people were present that warm July morning, all Japanese-American except for one black woman, but this church is in a Japanese-American neighborhood. The atmosphere was casual; people came in gradually and left from time to time to answer the telephone and so forth.

Over the altar was the *Omitama* (or *aramitama*), the PL emblem—a sun, represented here by a crystal mirror, with twenty-one gold rays, as the focus of worship. On each side of the altar were slogans in Japanese and English. The slogan for the year was "Year of great faith in PL," and the slogan for the month was "Be speedy in everything." In the latter, the English word "speedy," in Japanese writing, was used in the Japanese version as well as the English, though there are Japanese words with an equivalent meaning.

The service opened as a lovely young Japanese girl in a black cassock with violet scarf entered and went before the altar. She bowed and offered the *oyashikiri* gracefully. She then led in Japanese the long PL prayer. The official translation begins:

> Noble and merciful God, Mioya Okami,
> Thou hast created all things
> and dost make all things

> grow and develop ceaselessly
> in accord with Thy Divine Plan. . . .
>
> Thou hast revealed
> Thy way of Man as follows:
> "Be aware of all Creation
> and that nothing is nobler
> or more honorable than man,
> for he is the manifestation of God.
> Know that God hath created all things
> and that they follow
> their unique functions
> and fashion their true ways
> for the sake of mankind. . . ."
>
> I will earnestly follow
> Thy divine teachings, Mioshie,
> and express my true
> and sincere individuality
> in a life of art. . . .

Then came the daily morning prayer of PL followers:

> We . . . reverently speak in the presence of Mioya
> Okami and the spirits of our ancestors: We pray that You
> will favor and bless us with Your infinite glory, for we will
> live this day as children of God, not possessed by selfish-
> ness but showing forth our true individuality to live an
> artistic life.[45]

She then greeted the congregation, beginning with
"Thank you, Oshieoya-sama," thereby expressing gratitude
to the distant figure of Tokuchika Miki for the benefits he
brought them and the world. Then she talked about a carnival the church had sponsored a week before, when Japanese noodles had been sold to the neighborhood.

Next, two testimonial talks were given. Both were spo-

ken in Japanese and translated by the girl into English.
The first was by a young Japanese who had come over to
America sponsored by an American professional baseball
coach. The coach, a man kind and generous toward youth
of all races, had had nothing to do with religion. Later,
when the coach was dying, the young man said, he ad-
mitted that he wished he had something—faith, better
medicine—to help him. The PL member said he wished he
could have had more chances to talk with him about Perfect Liberty. He wished he had explained to him that life
is art and can be lived so that one feels nothing is left out,
and ends up as a completed, rounded expression.

Next, an elderly lady said that after working very hard
in the carnival she had heart palpitations. She called the
minister, who told her the palpitations were a *mishirase*.
She got *mioshie*, and accepted the *mishirase* as a warning
that she should live a more balanced life.

The sermon was by the young minister of the church,
who had been sent out from Japan. He wore a black cassock with a black-over-white collar, like a Japanese school
uniform. The sermon, based on the fifth precept, "Man
loses his true self when swayed by feelings or emotion,"
consisted mostly of stories of individual experiences. It is
typical of all the New Religions that they use largely anec-
dotal homilies, in contrast to the abstractly doctrinal lectures of traditional Buddhist temples and the moral addresses of Shinto.

The minister told of a child who was unruly in school.
The parents, PL members, contacted first their group
leader, then their minister. They got a *mioshie* which said
that the fault was with the parents; the mother had bad
feelings toward her mother-in-law. Next the minister told

of a child with squint eyes. In this case the child prayed the *oyashikiri* with the minister and was healed.

The service ended with another *oyashikiri*, and everyone saying heartily, "Thank you, Oshieoya-sama."

The most important worship service in PL is not the Sunday morning service, but the *hosho* ("treasure") service held on the twenty-first of each month, usually in the evening. On this occasion everyone is supposed to bring an offering placed in a special large white envelope. This is made into an important form of religious expression, and the envelope states that generous offerings bring generous blessings in many forms, and also help the international work of PL.

V

Before the war, the teachings of Hito no Michi spread to the Japanese-American community in the United States, but PL did not arrive until 1960, when several Japanese immigrants began missionary work in this country. Official incorporation as the "Church of Perfect Liberty" occurred in June. In 1961 a minister was sent out from Japan.

By 1974, American membership had grown to around five thousand, of whom 50 percent were Japanese, 25 percent Caucasian, 15 percent black, and 10 percent Spanish-American. PL has had far more success than any other religion of Japanese origin, except perhaps Nichiren Shoshu, in attracting members of black and Spanish-American backgrounds. There are six churches in the United States, and fifteen missions. The major strength is in the Los Angeles and San Francisco-Oakland areas.

The churches are governed by a ten-man board of directors elected by the congregation. The board meets monthly. The schedule of church activities is full: it includes art classes, tea ceremony classes, flower arrangement classes, language classes, services for the spirits of ancestors, and sports groups dedicated to hiking, golf, or bowling.

Sports are of special importance to PL. In Japan, the faith has sometimes been facetiously called the "golf religion" because of its practice of making golf links on the grounds of churches when feasible. This is related to its wholistic view of man, which insists that play or fun is a legitimate part of a balanced, artistic life, and that man is meant to be happy. It is also argued that sports promote personal and world peace, since it is better to expend aggressive and competitive drives on the playing field than elsewhere. In any case, it is not a religion solely of a "work ethic," but of a vigorous life in all dimensions of activity.

Other major events of PL in America are pilgrimages to the headquarters in Japan. Cultural festivals and the opening of new buildings or projects there provide occasions for groups going by chartered plane to Osaka to experience the splendor and hospitality of the faith in its heartland. Experiences like these, of course, are invaluable reinforcers of morale and commitment.

The year 1972 was an important one for PL in America. The church bought six hundred acres in the Santa Monica mountains near Los Angeles to establish a center comparable to the headquarters in Japan. Plans call for a temple, a hospital, a headquarters building, a golf course, and a community. The project raised local controversy because of opposition from conservation- and ecology-minded groups to development in these untouched hills, but PL seems determined to proceed. Doubtless the project will be of parklike quality. In any case, the matter brought considerable publicity to PL in newspapers and even in the national magazine *Newsweek*. In the previous year Marcus Bach, the well-known minister of the Unity movement and writer of popular books on religion, had published *The Power of Perfect Liberty,* a tribute to the faith which brought it before a wide American reading public.[46]

All these indications point in the direction of growth. Several internal steps were taken in 1972 to consolidate this position. The name was changed in America to simply "Perfect Liberty"—not, as before, PL Kyodan, PL Church, Perfect Liberty Order of America, or Church of Perfect Liberty.

An *oya*, Jiro Yano (father of the chief minister of the American work, Koreaki Yano) was sent from Japan to serve as spiritual director of the growing American work. According to a leaflet distributed by the church at that time, he can help the faithful in these ways:

1. He is able to give you MIOSHIE, Divine instruction, which helps you to change yourself for the better.
2. He is able to perform the rite of blessing which will cure illnesses and solve problems. Thousands have experienced these wonderful blessings.
3. He finds your true value and helps you to express your true self.
4. He guides you with the firm concept of God.
5. He has vast knowledge and experiences to solve your problems. For example, he knows:
   how to raise children
   how to accomplish your love
   how to be successful in business
   how to better human relationship
   how to bring about togetherness in the family
   how to live with peace of mind.[47]

Why do Occidentals join Perfect Liberty? Five themes appear to be predominant.

1. *The appeal of the "Life is Art" idea.* Like the New Thought churches, and like virtually all the New Religions of Japan, PL fundamentally has a mentalist, monistic world view. It is at pains to show that one's thinking underlies what happens to one. There is an explanation and something to blame (oneself) for what goes wrong. By the same token, the appeal of the Life is Art idea is that it gives to living the positive connotations of painting or architecture. It removes living from the realm of simple ethics or existential anxiety. Thus PL would in principle appeal to the same sort of people as does New Thought, with the added attraction of the beautiful word "art."

2. *The attraction of a faith almost wholly positive in image.* Because PL sanctifies health, sports, travel, and radiant happy faces, it seems a part of the world and self-image that many modern middle-class people, or people who like to think of themselves as middle-class, would like to have. Its organization of classes and groups devoted to cultural and sports activities makes it a total life center.

3. *The glamour of international connections.* A part of the appeal of all Japanese religions in America is the appeal of belonging to something cosmopolitan and exotic. Some Occidentals enjoy very much having friends of other nationalities, acquiring a second culture as well as a religion, symbolizing in this area of their life a love for Japan picked up perhaps through military service, business, or travel. The wonder of going to Japan on organized PL tours, being entertained as honored guests at the lavish PL buildings, and seeing brilliantly programmed pageants and services, playing golf with the smart girl "caddiettes" on the 36-hole course—all this makes the Asian religion a

marvelous new world, much more than just a place to go to church.

4. *The personal care that PL gives, especially in mioshie.* Very few if any other religions offer the individual as much personal attention in his spiritual life. Yet at the same time *mioshie* impersonalizes the attention in a way that makes getting guidance seem a natural, routine matter and images a highly efficient, knowledgeable organization. Asking for *mioshie* by mail does not have the "heavy" overtones of confession or pastoral counseling. This admirable balance, together with the very real support that PL ministers and above them the leaders of the movement offer, suits the needs of many. In short, the whole movement communicates the feeling to those drawn to it that someone who is highly competent in spiritual matters really cares about *me* and has a smoothly operating procedure to help me. All I need to do is "plug in" to it.

5. *Experience that it works.* The fundamental persuader for any conversion to a religious tradition very different from one's own, of course, has to be an experience or need powerful enough to overcome the ties of family, language, culture, and nation. It cannot depend on tradition, but must go against them as it tries to show a better way. For many who have entered Perfect Liberty, miraculous results from *oyashikiri* and *mioshie*—reinforced by the constantly presented testimonials of others—have provided some proof, and substantial change in their lives has done the rest.

In the summer of 1972 I interviewed an American black woman, Mrs. Eliseo Capellan, who had entered PL. She was originally Baptist, but married a Filipino and became a Roman Catholic. Back in 1966 she heard about PL from Filipino and Japanese friends who came to their house.

As soon as she inquired more about PL, people in the movement, she said, welcomed her eagerly, and the minister cared enough to look her up in the telephone book and call her. This greatly impressed her, and she also found the PL philosophy to be very attractive. More recently she was able to join a PL tour to Japan, on which she was treated royally and was deeply impressed with the work of the movement in Japan. She was especially struck favorably by the PL educational system in the headquarters —the alert and disciplined children, the school uniforms, the marvelous concerts and programs they presented. In this country she has been very active in the Head Start program and other community education activities, and says that what she admires most about the Catholic Church is its educational work. She wants PL to have a school at its new center in the Santa Monica mountains. (She also says that she is going back to the Catholic Church sometime, since one can be in PL and also in another church.)

VI

On October 21, 1972, a great *hosho*, or thanksgiving service, was held at the Ambassador Hotel in Los Angeles. At this service, which I attended, the first *oya* appointed to reside in the United States and give *mioshie* here rather than at long range from Japan was introduced to his flock. A large hall was needed to accommodate the crowd of a couple hundred or so. It seemed to me that it was about 75 percent Oriental and 25 percent Occidental, with at least as many blacks as Caucasians making up the Occidental contingent.

At the front of the hall the great PL emblem was set up as a focus of worship. To the accompaniment of dignified

march music on the piano, the eight or ten clerical offi-
ciants entered, garbed in striking white satin copes and
scapulars over dark-blue cassocks. The congregation recited the long PL prayer. The new *oya* for America presented a blessing by slowly doing the *oyashikiri,* then solemnly facing the congregation. The minister of each
church in America, and then representatives of the laity
of each, proceeded to the altar to offer a brief prayer for
this occasion. The special monthly offering was taken up.

After a short intermission came songs by a charming PL
children's choir. They sang several times a verse by Tokuchika Miki, officially translated: "Rejoice, I was born alone,
and may pass alone away; to leave my heart, Makoto my
virtuousness, Makoto my virtuousness, as my inheritance."

Then came three quite interesting testimonials, all by
Occidentals. The first was from a business executive who
has been prominent for some time in American PL affairs.
He said that he had spent his first eighteen years in
Seventh-day Adventist schools, where he was taught that
the greatest thing he could do would be to go to the Orient
and convert the Orientals from idols. He got away from
this, and went from religion to religion. Then, about four
years ago, he had met the Reverend Mr. Yano at the air-
port as he was coming to America, and they had discussed
PL. The new PL leader had told him to try it and see
for himself. He went to the PL church. At first the prayer-
symbol and so forth had seemed like "superstition." But
after concentrating on the Twenty-one Precepts, the
sounds of PL worship became less and less strange. The
Patriarch had said the most important thing is *makoto,*
and he found that philosophy easy. *Oyashikiri* was of great
benefit. By it, he said, he could multiply his capabilities
for the artistic life, for self-expression and for vigor, ten

times. He said he had sent several *mioshie* through headquarters, and now makes fewer mistakes. He concluded
by saying that since coming into PL he has been much
happier within himself.

A black woman said that several years ago she had been
suffering from severe headaches. A minister of PL had
come and offered the *oyashikiri* prayer, but still they didn't
go away. He asked her if she had ever received divine instruction (*mioshie*). She hadn't; he explained it to her,
saying that in three weeks she would receive the instructions. In the meantime, trouble that she had been having
with her husband kept getting worse, until one day her
husband said that he wanted them to separate. It was the
moment of crisis. Twenty minutes later the PL minister
called, saying that the divine instructions had arrived. He
came over, prayed with her, and delivered them. She was
led to realize that it was her bad thoughts, going back to
the time when her stepdaughter, whom she greatly re-
sented, had lived with them, which lay at the root of the
headaches. The minister told her to pray, following the
divine instructions, and forget the past. When she began
doing this sincerely, she had no more headaches. She re-
joiced that "now we have an *oya-sama* here with us," and
won't have to wait for divine instructions in the future.

A plainspoken young man addressed the group next. He
said he felt very fortunate to have been in PL for the last
few months. He said that he worked at a service station
as a mechanic. A lady minister of PL traded there and
lived across the street. He said that she had talked with
him several times about PL, and since she was a good cus-
tomer and neighbor, he tried to please her by giving her
the two-dollar initiation fee. She asked him what his

wishes were. He said peace of mind: he had been through two marriages and was a drunk. Almost immediately, and contrary to all expectations, he said, everything changed. He no longer desired drink, and was happy. He visited PL and read Bach's *The Power of Perfect Liberty*—it "got to him." He prayed for certain tools, and surprisingly got a whole new shop. He went to see his son, who was living in another community, and the visit was attended by many blessings—the principal of the boy's school, with whom he talked, could not help but notice how changed he was. Most remarkable of all, he prayed the *oyashikiri* prayer for his present fiancée, who had been missing for two months—and soon after she called him.

The evening ended with the formal introduction of the new *oya-sama*. He was presented with flowers by a young blonde, introduced by his son, the head of the American church, and was formally greeted by a prominent Occidental PL member.

To facilitate discussion, the latter asked him several questions. They were, with their answers:

1. *What does oya-sama mean?* It means one whose job is to help people. He is trained to determine the *cause* of sickness and unhappiness in people.

2. *What is mioshie?* It is instruction, given by one who teaches in place of God, as to *why* misfortune happens. Misfortune is not *caused* by God. Rather, we take it as a *divine warning*. Through *mioshie* you can find the mistakes *you* have made in your daily life.

3. *How is it possible to know the cause?* Everyone is endowed with power to tell the cause of what happens to him. But because the *oya-sama* has been trained under strict guidance, he is empowered with direct intuition,

though this is just a sharpening of his natural powers. This power is the same as the wisdom of God. "You too can have it. Come study with me!"

4. *Is it true that you have great personal powers to heal and guide?* It is true. People who have come here tonight will all be saved. But you must have strong, unblemished desire. This is *makoto*.

5. *PL has recently purchased six hundred acres for a headquarters, golf course, medical center, and so forth. What is the purpose of this?* The basic concept is that life must be happy and cannot be unhappy. Bettering cultural facilities is a minute example of building up the capital of art.

In the talk that followed, the *oya* said that the most important thing in life is oneself. Above all, it is necessary to understand one's own existence. "We are here to take away all the unhappiness in America!"

There could be no better theme on which to end this section, for that is indeed the purpose and mood of Perfect Liberty.

READING SELECTION

The following passage is from a translation published by PL of some lines from Tokuchika Miki's basic book, Jinsei wa Geijutsu dearu *("Human Life is Art"). They express some fundamental points of his philosophy.*

PL Kyodan is a religious order that teaches under the motto of "Life is Art."

Generally speaking, we may define art simply as "Something expressing the individuality of its creator through an object." When an artist happens to become blessed with some inspiration, he gives it expression in a form specific to his profession. The finer the works of art, the greater the individuality of the artist that permeates them. Therefore, a conscientious artist, when engaging in artistic creation, completely devotes himself to his work, does not think of position, honor, or money, and makes extraordinary efforts even at the risk of his life. After having taken such great pains he succeeds in creating an object of art. In this process of creation he feels spiritual pleasure akin to religious exaltation. This is because he takes delight in expressing his own individuality through creating an object of art.

But is such pleasure a privilege of professional artists only? No, it is not. Art consists in expressing one's own individuality through an object. Man can express his individuality in every act he does. In cooking food, in sweeping a room, in making tea, in nurturing a child, in stocking merchandise, in displaying merchandise in a store, in selling it to customers, in negotiating a loan, in digging up coal, in raising crops, in engaging in education, social welfare work or politics—all people engaged in all kinds of professions in this world can express their respective individuality every day in all matters handled by them, from moment to moment.

There is nothing in human affairs that cannot become art. Man's life begins and ends in self expression. It is just a series of artistic creation. Life is Art.

—"Quotation of Oshieoya," *PL: A Modern Religion for Modern Man,* booklet (PL Kyodan, n.d.), pp. 10–11.

7

The Japanese New Religions and American Culture

In exploring the world of Japanese New Religions in America, we have found a double cultural exchange. The New Religions arose in Japan partly as a result of the stimulus of contact with the West. They embodied the response of many Japanese to the slow disintegration of a traditional, integral, hierarchical society. They expressed the modern need for religious structures capable of handling the new, acute discovery of one's isolated subjectivity. Even though they retained and revitalized themes of traditional Japanese religion, far more than ordinary Buddhism and Shinto they state and propagate them in a modern, half-westernized manner. They bespeak the modern goals of affluence, progress, and attaining authentic self-identity in a fractured world.

Yet, when they first came to America, the New Religions appeared as Eastern visitors, attractive but very alien islands of kimonos, gongs, eight-legged altars, and outlandish mystical doctrines. As time went on, they became American, not because the religions themselves changed but more because they came to be understood by some as genuinely meeting needs of Americans that were unfulfilled by American culture. Thus they have a place in the

America of the last half of the twentieth century as properly as the 1976 Bicentennial.

All through history, the bringing together of diverse cultural backgrounds has been the wellspring of new advances. The civilization of India, and of Hinduism and Buddhism in their classical forms, is the product of the marriage of the virile Indo-European culture of the ancient Aryan invaders and the soft, mystical world of the indigenous Dravidian farmers. Christianity, and the civilization of medieval and modern Europe shaped by it, reflects the interaction of Greek and Hebrew world views.

Today, the discovery of the East by the West has contributed to the brightening dawn of a new world view which is bound to grow in importance as we move toward the twenty-first century. Its outriders are everywhere: on campuses, in the human potential movement, in scientific philosophy, in popular books from *The Greening of America* to *Jonathan Livingston Seagull*.

The new world view is basically a mystical monism, a belief that all is unified and that all, especially human consciousness, is an expression of the divine mind directly, which is as old as Plato, or Vedanta in India. But it is reinforced by a new mood in science, adumbrated by Einstein and expressed in the scientific Vedanta of Carl von Weiszäcker and the Nobel Prize-winning Erwin Schrödinger, who have stressed the necessary unity of all parts of the cosmos, the necessary interaction of mind with a "material" universe which is really an energy field full of indeterminacies and half created by the relationship of object and observer. New breakthroughs in psychical research, such as the work of Cleve Backster on the ability of plants to respond telepathically to thoughts and emotions, alluded to in connection with World Messianity's nature farming, add to the new world view's profound sense of the mysterious interdependency of matter, mind, and sense.

Changes in the fabric of society have doubtless contributed to the incoming of the new world view too, for the unconsciously felt needs of a society and the types of scientific and philosophical discoveries it makes always have no small relationship. It is interesting to note that, historically, mystical world views tend to emerge in urbanizing, overpopulated societies, where opportunity for geographical expansion has been exhausted. One thinks of Benares, Loyang, Alexandria. When a society sees itself as having reached its outward limits, then the exploration of "inner space" becomes more and more important. Even as the necessary increasing regimentation of the social organization depersonalizes the individual outwardly, he enhances his sense of subjective individuality and infinity through heightening his mystical, psychic, and sensuous awareness.

Religion of the traditional Judeo-Christian sort, on the other hand, with its monotheistic High God working through history in the acts of men and nations, is connected with nomadic and geographically expansive societies. Its covenant, or even marriage, model of the relationship between man and a God who is other than man, though with whom man can have deep relationships of obedience, agreement, and love, suggests the relationship of businesslike, active, and loving adults in an open society, not that of a mystic with the depths of his self. The emergence of the new mysticism indicates more than anything else a far-reaching change in Western man's awareness of himself, and thus of the metaphors to which he instinctively turns for an understanding of how he is related to his ultimate environment, the Infinite.

The new world view posits that we and all that is are units of a cosmic field in which matter and consciousness interface everywhere. The goal of life is to realize oneself as an expression of the universal sea of consciousness, of which one is a part as a bay is part of the ocean, bound to it by a network of countless currents, tides, and undertows: all this can be grasped without word or logic in a timeless surge of open ecstasy, a "peak experience," whether induced by meditation, creative work, sensitivity to another's body, or "high play." Ancient symbols of the universe as a balanced harmony of parts have been revived to visualize what is felt: the kabbalistic tree, the mandala.

The discovery of the religions of the East has been important to this development. Vedanta, Zen, and yoga have been no small part of the experience of many makers of the new consciousness. The Eastern religions have been found to put with daring conviction the suggestion of Western mystics, poets, and seekers that God is really "within," or at least that by intensifying awareness of one's inner weather, one can find the path of the spiritual ascent. Thus, for many, Eastern vocabulary, art, and symbols—as well as practices—provide far more eloquent signposts for the spiritual life as they actually experience it than do Western.

The New Religions of Japan are only a part of the East-West spiritual rapprochement, but in some respects they are especially significant. The very fact that they often sound halfway between East and West, rather than full-blown expressions of mystical monism of the classical Eastern sort, makes them eloquent of the spiritual ferment of modern times. Even though their still-nascent intellectual expression may sometimes sound unpolished compared to the mighty philosophies of classical Hinduism and Buddhism, we recognize in them authentic tones of the modern experience, and hence we can reverberate to what they are saying specifically as moderns, caught between one age and another. Traditional Hinduism and Buddhism are smooth and rounded and deep-glowing as vessels of burnished brass, but one recognizes, however sadly and reluctantly, that their profundity is the perfection of completion, and that they are slipping into the past. While symbols drawn from them, as we have seen, are still potent, revolution, rapid social change, and ways of life radically different from those of their great periods have increasingly left them, in both East and West, the possessions only of those happy ones for whom the past is as real as the present.

Of course, the New Religions of Japan are in a real sense conservative reactions to modernity, and this may inhibit their future effectiveness. They follow tradition in using religious language and symbols at all to express subjective sensitivity. They are concerned with reconciling isolated, alienated moderns to their cultural past in Japan and—as we have seen in the case of Nichiren Shoshu—in America.

But what they express in this language is the experience of modernity and a perception that we are between one age and another. Talk of the New Age, the Third Civilization, and so forth, all indicates an awareness of powerful changes afoot.

The New Religions, as expressers of modernity, almost repeat—though in dulcet and indirect tones—the blasphemous-sounding words of Nietzsche as he stated, more forcefully than many wished to hear, such phrases as: "God is dead" . . . "Remain true to the earth" . . . "I teach you the Superman" . . . "The Superman shall be the meaning of the earth."

For, while they certainly believe in a living monotheistic or monistic deity, for them at least the traditional Judeo-Christian God has been surpassed, and the deity who has spoken for our times through their recent founders and prophets is concerned mainly that man be true to the earth. It is here that a paradise is being created as the New Age unfolds, and a new kind of man is being brought to birth who is capable of constructing and appreciating the New Earth, and our most meaningful immortality (through reincarnation) is nowhere but here.

There is much room for dialogue between the New Religions and the Judeo-Christian tradition, as well as between them and the American cultural crisis. In the past, Christianity has been both more questioning and more hopeful than Eastern religions. Insofar as it has regarded man as just a creature made by God, and a "fallen" one at that, it has been highly dubious of talk of an inner identity of man with God, fearing that those who inflate themselves with such notions are likely to end up worse than those who are content with a more modest view of their relation to their Source, one simply of obedience and love. At its best, believing that man not being divine is always fallible and capable of falling into egotistic follies, this tradition questions whether any human teaching, philosophy, belief in spiritual advancement or spiritual technique can be absolutized as "the one answer." A sometimes gloomy dread of intellectual idolatry, suspicious of those who seem to be too much "at ease in Zion," lies behind the restless, driven, guilt-ridden, yet immensely creative style of being human out of which the goods and the evils alike of Western civilization have spawned.

Yet, besides being more questioning, the Western tradition is also more hopeful than the classical Eastern. It makes central a progressive view of God's working in time, beginning with the creation, moving through successively more expansive acts of God on behalf of man—the exodus from Egypt, the incarnation of God in Christ—leading up to the greatest event of all, the descent of the heavenly Jerusalem to earth and the making of a new heaven and a new earth. If Christianity is a difficult religion to believe, it also makes the greatest promises!

But at least on a secular level, in recent centuries this progressivistic schema of man's experience in time has proved not only believable, but when believed, self-fulfilling—it is expressed in the pioneer belief in the conquest of new land, the capitalist belief in expanding affluence, the humanistic belief in scientific progress, the Marxist belief in a historical process leading through revolution to a paradisal society.

Traditional Eastern religions have, one might say, started with more and ended with less. These statements are oversimplified, but do represent tendencies and attitudes. Presuming that man's true nature is identity with the Absolute, and that this is always true though man may be unaware of his true nature, they have not used the rhetoric of rebellion, guilt, and fallenness to articulate the human condition, but only that of ignorance, sloth, and deluded attachments. Yet on the other hand they have not viewed irreversible historical progress or world transformation by divine action as religious goals so much as individual "isolation" of one's true nature as the Absolute, a goal an individual may attain while the outside world, beginningless and endless, continues its hollow dance much as before.

But the New Religions of Japan start with more and end with more. All through them breathes an optimistic image of man's nature, one attuned to a very sanguine reading of Buddhist, Taoist, and Confucian doctrine. There is little of the dark and tragic tones of the classic Western image so powerfully expressed by Dante and Milton. Yet they *also* present a future-oriented hope similar to that of the Judeo-Christian tradition. They too look for a new heaven and a new earth, or at least a new earth, with a new kind of humanity in it.

Here indeed is scope for dialogue. If they challenge the pessimism about man's nature of the West, they also challenge the historical pessimism of the East. They imply that both run counter to something modernity has discovered about human nature. They would say that both create false dualisms between religious commitment and the possibilities of the present. The Western view perhaps ends in the neuroses and anxieties of battle between man's ideals and his nature, between spirit and flesh, as it imposes on him blacker and brighter colors than he can bear without a heaven which robs him of his calling to be true to the earth. The Eastern view, they might say, does offer the integration of the self, but only at frightful cost to other legitimate human hopes and desires.

The older religions, of course, can respond by saying that optimism is its own worst enemy if it is too shallow and sanguine, and refuses to accept those final limitations which are part of man's nature, and that none is more wretched in the end than he who was too soon uncautiously hopeful.

It is enough for now to state that, whatever the upshot

of the dialogue, the New Religions of Japan as they are
represented in America are a part of the American religious future. They present clearly and simply a very real
insight—that man's God, his hope, and his paradise must
be true to the modern understanding of man as a growing,
expansive, and future-oriented being who is a psychosomatic unity of mind and body. It is time they and the
faiths of the West exchanged experiences and insights at
the deepest level.

Addresses of Groups

The following 1974 American addresses of groups discussed in this book are provided for the assistance of readers who may wish to obtain further information about any of them.

TENRIKYO
   The Tenrikyo Mission Headquarters in America
   2727 East First Street
   Los Angeles, California 90033

NICHIREN SHOSHU OF AMERICA
   Nichiren Shoshu of America
   1351 Ocean Front
   Santa Monica, California 90401

CHURCH OF WORLD MESSIANITY
   Church of World Messianity
   3068 San Marino Street
   Los Angeles, California 90006

SEICHO-NO-IE
   Seicho-no-Ie Church
   14527 S. Vermont Avenue
   Gardena, California 90247

PERFECT LIBERTY
 Perfect Liberty, North America
 700 South Adams Street
 Glendale, California 91205

Notes

1. See my *Religious and Spiritual Groups in Modern America* (Prentice-Hall, Inc., 1973), pp. 255–262, for information on Zen in America.

2. Harry Thomsen, *The New Religions of Japan* (Tokyo and Rutland, Vermont: Charles E. Tuttle Company, 1963).

3. In this book Japanese names are always written in the Western manner, with given name first and surname last.

4. Ichiro Hori, *Folk Religion in Japan: Continuity and Change,* ed. by Joseph M. Kitagawa and Alan L. Miller (The University of Chicago Press, 1968). See especially Chapter VI, "The New Religions and the Survival of Shamanic Tendencies."

5. See my *One Way: The Jesus Movement and Its Meaning* (Prentice-Hall, Inc., 1973).

6. *Life of Oyasama, The Foundress of Tenrikyo* (Manuscript Edition, Tenri, Japan: Tenrikyo Church Headquarters, Trial Edition, 1967), p. 307. *Sah* is an exclamatory term roughly equivalent to "Oh."

7. *Mikagura-uta* (Tenri, Japan: Tenrikyo Church Headquarters, 1972), p. 5.

8. *Ofudesaki: The Tip of the Divine Writing Brush* (Tenri, Japan: The Headquarters of Tenrikyo Church, preliminary edition, 1971), I: 21–28, pp. 8–9.

9. *Ofudesaki,* I: 13–17, pp. 6–7.

10. *Ofudesaki*, I: 1–3, p. 3

11. *Life of Oyasama*, pp. 303, 304.

12. Walter Pennington, "Certain Aspects of Tenrikyo," in *Tenrikyo: Its History and Teachings* (Tenri, Japan: Tenrikyo Overseas Mission Department, 1966), pp. 235–240.

13. Forest E. Barber, "The Seeker and the Quest," in *ibid.*, pp. 241–255.

14. Sakyamuni is a title meaning "Sage of the Sakya tribe," the family to which the Buddha belonged. This is the historical Gautama Buddha ("Gautama" is a proper name; "Buddha" is a title meaning "Enlightened One") from whose experience and teaching all forms of Buddhism ultimately derive. He is usually dated by scholars approximately 563–483 B.C.

15. H. Kern (tr.), *Saddharma-Puṇḍarīka or The Lotus of the True Law* (Dover Publications, Inc., 1963. Originally published by The Clarendon Press, Oxford, 1884, as Vol. XXI of "The Sacred Books of the East"), pp. 213–214.

16. *World Tribune*, Oct. 16, 1972, p. 7.

17. *Seikyo Times*, Jan. 1972, pp. 18–29.

18. Press release, Nichiren Shoshu of America, Nov. 1972.

19. *NSA Seminar Report 1968–1971* (Santa Monica: World Tribune Press, 1972), Appendix 3, "NSA Demographics," pp. 93–106. The age breakdown statistics have, in consultation with an NSA official, been slightly modified to make them equal 100 percent.

20. *Newsweek*, June 5, 1972, p. 68.

21. See Peter Tompkins and Christopher Bird, *The Secret Life of Plants* (Harper & Row, Publishers, Inc., 1973). In medieval Buddhism, a major topic of discussion was whether plants are "sentient beings" and hence capable of realizing Buddhahood.

22. *Bulletin of World Messianity/Johrei Fellowship*, Vol. II, No. 5 (May 1972), pp. 6–7.

23. *Sounds of the Dawn*, Vol. I (Atami, Japan: Church of World Messianity, 1971), pp. 20–21.

24. *Sounds of the Dawn,* Vol. I, p. 48.

25. *Teachings of Meishu-sama,* Vol. I, rev. ed. (Atami, Japan: Church of World Messianity, 1965, 1967), p. 28.

26. *Teachings of Meishu-sama,* Vol. I, p. 47.

27. *Teachings of Meishu-sama,* Vol. I, p. 54.

28. Masaharu Taniguchi, "What Is Shinsokan? How to Practice?" (Leaflet, n.d.)

29. Roy Eugene Davis, *Miracle Man of Japan* (Lakemont, Georgia: CSA Press, 1970), pp. 14–15.

30. H. Neill McFarland, *The Rush Hour of the Gods* (Harper & Row, Publishers, Inc., 1970), p. 149. C. B. Offner and H. Van Straelen, *Modern Japanese Religions* (Leiden: E. J. Brill, 1963), p. 72.

31. Davis, *Miracle Man of Japan,* pp. 24–25.

32. Seicho-no-Ie America Sokatsubu, "'Miracle Man of Japan': Dr. Masaharu Taniguchi & SEICHO-NO-IE." (Leaflet, n.d.)

33. Masaharu Taniguchi, *Divine Education and Spiritual Training of Mankind* (Tokyo: Seicho-no-Ie Foundation, 1956), p. 143.

34. These are published on the inside front cover of every issue of the magazine *Seicho-no-Ie.*

35. Masaharu Taniguchi, *Recovery from All Diseases* (Tokyo: Seicho-no-Ie Foundation, 1963), pp. 93–95.

36. Masaharu Taniguchi, *Recovery from All Diseases,* pp. 102–105.

37. Masaharu Taniguchi, *Divine Education and Spiritual Training of Mankind,* pp. 27–28.

38. Fenwicke L. Holmes and Masaharu Taniguchi, *The Science of Faith* (Tokyo: Nippon Kyobun-sha Co., Ltd., 1962).

39. McFarland, *The Rush Hour of the Gods,* p. 125.

40. Offner and Van Straelen, *Modern Japanese Religions,* p. 83.

41. Offner and Van Straelen, *Modern Japanese Religions,* pp. 84–85.

42. Thomsen, *The New Religions of Japan,* p. 136.

43. Miki Tokuchika, *Jinsei wa Geijutsu dearu* (Toyko: Dai-Nihon Insha, 1960, 1970).

44. Church of Perfect Liberty, North America, *Oyashikiri: PL Guidance No. 2.* (Pamphlet, n.d.)

45. Church of Perfect Liberty, *The PL Prayer.* (N.d.)

46. Marcus Bach, *The Power of Perfect Liberty* (Prentice-Hall, Inc., 1971).

47. Perfect Liberty, *Oyasama.* (Pamphlet, n.d.)

Index

Amatsu Norito, 120, 122, 137, 138–139, 143

Buddhism, 14, 15, 20, 27–29, 69–110, 120, 156, 185, 210, 213

Christ, 25, 57, 126–127, 156, 177
Christianity, 56–58, 59, 124, 126–127, 157, 162, 207–209, 211
Confucianism, 25, 30, 31, 185, 191, 213
Consciousness of Beauty, 111, 132–133

"Dancing Religion." *See* Odori Shukyo
Deguchi, Nao, 21
Deguchi, Onisaburo, 21, 24, 123, 154, 185–186

Esho funi (inner and outer not separate), 74, 82, 105

Gedatsu, 13
Gohonzon, 69, 75, 87–88, 100
Gongyo, 70, 74

Hito no Michi, 32, 181–182, 195
Holmes, Fenwicke, 155–156

Iburi, Izo, 52
Ikeda, Daisaku, 93–94, 96–97, 99

Japanese-Americans, 13, 34, 35, 65, 100–101, 112, 141
Johrei, 31, 111–119, 121, 122, 125, 132, 137, 144

Kamakura period, 19–20, 84
Kanada, Tokumitsu, 178–181
Kannon, 120, 122–123, 147
Kanrodai, 46, 65
Karma, 28–29, 45
Kawate, Bunjiro, 17, 24
Komeito political party, 95
Konjin, 17
Konko Daijin. *See* Kawate, Bunjiro
Konkokyo, 13, 17
Kyoshu-sama, 128, 138

Lotus Sutra, 20, 81–83, 85–86

Makiguchi, Tsunesaburo, 89–90
Mappo (last age), 84–85

Meishu-sama. *See* Okada, Mo-kichi
Mikagura Uta, 40, 42, 61, 67
Miki, Tokuchika, 181–182, 193, 201, 204–205
Miki, Tokuharu, 180–182
Min-on, 79–80, 92, 99
Mioshie (divine instruction), 183, 189–190, 194, 197, 199
Mishirase (divine warning), 189–190, 194
Mitake-kyo, 179

Nakayama, Miki, 17, 37–40, 47–53, 64–65
Nam Myoho Renge Kyo, 20, 70, 71, 75, 86–87, 104
Nature farming, 111, 112, 117–120, 128, 130, 132
New Age, 16, 25, 31, 46, 79, 87–88, 93–94, 112, 127, 131, 137
New Religions of Japan
  classifications, 16
  common characteristics, 23–32
New Thought, 155–156, 159, 162, 165–166
Nichiren, 16, 19–20, 83–89
Nichiren Shoshu, 16, 31, 32, 34, 36, 69–110
  conventions, 76, 107–110
  doctrine, 77–79, 80–87, 103–106
  head temple. *See* Sho-Hondo
  history in America, 96–101
  history in Japan, 89–94
  membership, 75, 79, 91, 101–102
  organization, 106
  temples, 100

testimonials, 72–76, 98–99
worship, 69–75
Nidai-sama, 128

Obon, 19, 51
Odori Shukyo, 13
Ofudesaki (Omoto scripture), 21
Ofudesaki (Tenrikyo scripture), 43, 45, 47–48, 51, 57, 62, 67–68
Okada, Mokichi, 22, 32, 111, 116, 119, 120–128, 131–132, 134–136, 138–139, 145–146
Omoto, 16, 21–23, 120–122, 154, 172, 185–186
Osazuke, 54
Oshieoya, 181, 183, 190, 193

Perfect Liberty, 16, 22, 31, 32, 36, 178–205
  doctrine, 184–190
  emblem, 192
  history in America, 195–197
  history in Japan, 178–184
  hosho (thanksgiving service), 195, 200–204
  "Life is Art" concept, 184, 185–190, 198, 204–205
  membership, 184, 195, 200
  Occidental converts, 195, 198–203
  organization, 195–196
  reasons for appeal, 198–199
  testimonials, 194–195, 201–203
  Twenty-one Precepts, 184–185
  worship, 190–195, 200–204
Pure Land Buddhism, 20, 49

Reikai Monogatari ("Tales of the Spirit World"), 21, 22, 121, 123, 154
Reincarnation, 28, 45, 60, 62, 136, 172
Reiyukai, 20
Rissho Kosei Kai, 20

Sacred Focal Point, 124, 125, 137
Sadanaga, Masayasu. *See* Williams, George M.
Seicho-no-Ie, 16, 31, 32, 36, 147–177
  declaration, 161
  doctrine, 149, 159–161, 175–176
  history in America, 166–167
  history in Japan, 157–159
  laughing practice, 150
  membership, 165–166
  Occidental converts, 147–150, 165, 174–175
  organization, 166–168
  scripture, 151, 157, 168
  testimonials, 150–151, 162–164, 169–170
  training sessions, 170–174
  worship, 150–153, 168–170
Shamanism, 23–24, 31, 179–180
Shingon, 23, 85, 179–181, 185
Shinsokan, 31, 148, 151–152, 168, 171, 173–174, 176
Shinto, 14, 25, 35, 37, 39, 65–66, 90, 103, 139, 171, 179, 194
Shinto-Tokumitsu-kyo, 180–181
Sho-Hondo, 71–72, 88
Sokagakkai, 20, 32, 89–93, 95, 96, 97, 100, 103
Spiritualism, 15, 136

Taniguchi, Masaharu, 22, 148, 150, 151, 153–159, 162–167, 169, 175, 176–177
Taoism, 17, 25, 185, 213
Tenchi-kane-no-kami, 17
Tendai, 85
Tenri City, 11, 25, 53–55, 59, 64
Tenrikyo, 11–12, 13, 16, 17, 28, 31, 32, 36, 37–68
  creation story, 43–44, 65
  doctrine, 42–46, 60–63, 64
  ethics, 62
  founding, 48–52
  history in America, 55–56
  history in Japan, 48–53
  membership, 56
  Occidental converts, 56, 58–63, 66–67
  organization, 63–64
  scripture. *See* *Ofudesaki* (Tenrikyo scripture)
  testimonials, 54, 58–63
  worship, 37–41, 46, 58, 61
Toda, Josei, 89–93
Tokugawa period, 18, 48–49

Williams, George M., 97–98, 100
World Messianity, 16, 31, 32, 36, 111–146, 207
  doctrine, 131–137
  headquarters, 115
  healing, 124–125
  history in America, 129–131
  history in Japan, 120–129
  membership, 111–112, 130
  organization, 128–129, 137–138
  worship, 137–141
World Tribune, 75, 80, 87–88, 98, 99, 100

Yamabushi, 23–24, 49, 179–180   Yokigurashi, 41, 43, 44–45, 59
Yano, Jiro, 197, 203–204   Yukon, 134–135
Yoboku, 54
Yoga, 209   Zen, 12, 23, 41, 178, 209